RAISING YOUR VIBRATION

Fine Tune Your Body & Soul to Receive Messages from Heaven

KEVIN HUNTER

WARRIOR
OF LIGHT
PRESS
Los Angeles, California

Warrior of Light Press
www.kevin-hunter.com

Body, Mind & Spirit/Angels & Guides
Inspiration & Personal Growth

PRODUCTION CREDITS:
Project Editor: James Szopo

Content in *Raising Your Vibration* is taken from the books, *Warrior of Light: Messages from my Guides and Angels*, *Empowering Spirit Wisdom* and *Darkness of Ego*.

Acknowledgements

Thank you to my spiritual posse that consists of God and my personal sports team of Angels, Guides, Archangels and Saints. Thank you also Archangel Gabriel, Archangel Uriel and Archangel Raphael.

Warrior of Light
mini-book pocket series

Spirit Guides and Angels:
How I Communicate with Heaven

Soul Mates and Twin Flames:
Attracting in Love, Friendships and the Human Heart

Divine Messages for Humanity:
Channeled Communication from the Other Side on Death, the
Afterlife, the Ego, Prejudices, Prayer and the Power of Love

Raising Your Vibration:
Fine Tune Your Body & Soul to Receive Messages from Heaven

Connecting with the Archangels

The Seven Deadly Sins
A Modern Day Interpretation of Humanity's Toxic Challenges
with a Practical Spiritual Twist

Chapters

A Word

Raising Your Vibration is a mini-pocket book and part of a series of *Warrior of Light* books. Some of the content in the mini-pocket books are disbursed throughout three of the bigger *Warrior of Light* books called: *Warrior of Light: Messages from my Guides and Angels, Empowering Spirit Wisdom* and *Darkness of Ego.* The exception is the book, *The Seven Deadly Sins.* The bigger *Warrior of Light* books contain a variety of information within the spiritual empowerment genre. The reason behind releasing five separate mini-pocket books is for those who just want to read about one specific topic and are not interested in the rest. For example, all content soul mate love and relationship related would be in the mini-pocket book called, *Soul Mates and Twin Flames.* Rather than having to buy all three big books to read about the information in each of them, you have it all in one mini-pocket book.

Author's Note

All *Warrior of Light* books are infused with practical messages and guidance that my Spirit team has taught and shared with me revolving around many different topics. The main goal is to fine tune your body, mind and soul. This improves humanity one person at a time. You are a Divine communicator and perfectly adjusted and capable of receiving messages from Heaven. This is for your benefit in order to live a happier, richer life. It is your individual responsibility to respect yourself and this planet while on your journey here.

The messages and information enclosed in this and all of the *Warrior of Light* books may be in my own words, but they do not come from me. They come from God, the Holy Spirit, my Spirit team of guides, angels and sometimes certain Archangels and Saints. I am merely the liaison or messenger in delivering and interpreting the intentions of what they wish to communicate. They love that I talk about them and share this stuff as it gets other people to work with them too!

There is one main hierarchy Saint who works with me leading the pack. His name is Nathaniel. He is often brutally truthful and forceful, as he does not mince words. There may be topics in this and my other books that might bother you or make you uncomfortable. He asks that you examine the underlying cause of this discomfort and come to terms with the fear attached. He cuts right to the heart of humanity without apology. I have learned quite a bit from him while adopting his ideology, which is Heaven's philosophy as a whole.

I am one with the Holy Spirit and have many Spirit Guides and Angels around me. As my connections to the other side grew to be daily over the course of my life, more of them joined in behind the others. I have often seen, sensed, heard and been privy to the dozens of magnificent lights that crowd around me on occasion.

If I use the word "He" when pertaining to God, this does not mean that I am advocating that he is a male. Simply replace the word, "He" with one you are comfortable using to identify God for you to be. This goes for any gender I use as examples. When I say, "spirit team", I am referring to a team of 'Guides and Angels'. The purpose of the *Warrior of Light* books is to empower and help you improve yourself, your life and humanity as a whole. It does not matter if you are a beginner or well versed in the subject matter. There may be something that reminds you of something you already know or something that you were unaware of. We all have much to share with one another, as we are all one in the end. This book and all of the *Warrior of Light* series of books contain information and directions on how to reach the place where you can be a fine tuned instrument to receive your own messages from your own Spirit team.

Some of my personal stories are infused and sprinkled in the books. This is in order for you to see how it works effectively for me. With some of my methods, I hope that you gain insight, knowledge or inspiration. It may prompt you to recall incidents where you were receiving heavenly messages in your own life. There are helpful ways that you can improve your existence and have a connection with Heaven throughout this book. Doing so will greatly transform yourself in all ways allowing you to attract wonderful circumstances at higher levels and live a happier more content life.

~ Kevin Hunter

Raising Your
Vibration

Chapter One

FINE TUNING YOUR SOUL

*H*ow do I receive messages from my guides and angels? This is a complex question since every soul's methods vary. Souls connect with Heaven in a myriad of ways. Laying it all out in a step by step manner does not always work for some. The ways suggested could be too confusing or intermediate for those who do not consider to being in the advanced class. Those who are brand new at diving in at expanding their consciousness and raising their vibration have poured in requests that some basics be discussed. *Raising Your Vibration* is the beginner's class on picking up some of the immediate guidance to consider implementing in order to improve your soul and state of mind in this material driven physical world. One of the big inquiries others desire is to communicate with the other side in order to know what their future holds. Even if you are able to connect, this does not mean your future will be relayed to you. Your spirit team of guides and angels do not live your life for you. What is relayed to you is on a need to know basis that will enrich and grow your soul.

For example, you might become frustrated when years have gone by and yet the love relationship you desire has not been forthcoming. For certain circumstances, there are pieces to the puzzle that need to be maneuvered on your behalf before what you crave happens. There is an excess of possible reasons that could come forth as to why there is no love partner in someone's life. Each case would need to be studied individually.

Every soul is communicating with the other side whether they're aware of it or not. I could be walking from my car to the elevators in a corporate building and Spirit messages are sifting through me mostly via clairaudience *(clear hearing)* or claircognizance *(clear knowing)*. I'm not doing anything specific to make it happen. Nor am I attempting to conduct a psychic reading, or asking my Spirit team questions as I hurriedly walk to my appointment. The messages naturally fall into my vicinity without me wanting it or thinking about it. It's always been this way and it's all I've ever known. I was born with one foot in this world and the other in the spirit world. All souls who do not feel they have this ability can get back to that space by making healthy life changes. You were born connecting with the other side, but somewhere along the way blocks were formed.

One of the big ways of connecting with Spirit is by raising your vibration. Fortune telling psychic readings or someone with enhanced psychic abilities are unlike raising your vibration. Someone who is psychically gifted could have a low vibration or operate from ego, but they are still exceptional at connecting with spirit effortlessly. Raising your vibration is important for your soul's growth beyond becoming more psychic.

Your vibration is an invisible energy field that exists within the DNA of your soul, aura, and physical body. It is energy that would be seen by someone with heightened clairvoyance *(clear seeing)* or sensed through clairsentience *(clear feeling)*. If Archangels and Angels are God's arms and hands, then your "vibration" is your soul's arms and hands. Your vibration is made up of undetectable cells to the human eye. These cells fluctuate and change colors depending on your mood, your thought processes, who you surround yourself with, as well as what you ingest into your body among many other "negative" things.

Your soul and entire aura is an everlasting breathing energy field that has an effect on your state of mind. This is whether you desire to be happy in your Earthly life or miserable. A chief executive officer of a major corporation is an angry curmudgeon who is rude to the staff and only interested in making money in any way they can. This person might be financially successful, but they are still perpetually miserable and a spiritual failure. This angry state lowers their vibration which brings in an onslaught of negative circumstances and health issues at some point in their life. This is due to the angry stressed state they've endured throughout the course of their human existence. It builds up like mold in a damp basement, until the individual decides to eradicate it and make some healthy lifestyle changes. The changes put into practice would be with the objective of raising your vibration. When your vibration is high, you feel euphoric feelings of joy, love, peace and contentment. You discover that what you desire moves into your vicinity much more fluidly. If something has not been forthcoming, in a high vibrational state you are not bothered by that in the slightest. You operate from the space of being totally centered and together. The abundance that falls into your vicinity is your soul operating in its high vibrational state.

You are in a temporary physical body with an inflated ego that enjoys pushing you to experiencing negative feelings, such as anger or sadness, when a life circumstance throws you a curve ball. This can seem inevitable depending on the kind of life you live and who you surround yourself with. When you have felt and expressed negative feelings in the past, you may be able to point out that while in that state you were not thinking clearly. This might have prompted you to react harshly towards someone else, or you reacted impulsively by making a decision you later wish you could take back. The ego is your lower self which puts you in a state of removal from your higher self. It's almost like an out of body experience. You lose all logic while in that lower self state. This affects how you communicate to others and the choices you make.

You could be a busy professional who works a job that drains your soul's life force; therefore working a job you despise will lower your vibration. You sit in traffic to get to this job you're unhappy at, only to leave at the end of the day and sit in traffic to get home. This stress in driving in those conditions lowers your vibration.

You are made up of energy as every living organism, plant, animal, element, atom vibrates of energy. When you take a stroll through a garden or park alone, many sense a heavy weight being lifted off them. You suddenly feel a little elated and more relaxed. This is an example of what it might feel like as your vibration begins to rise. But then you get a phone call from a friend who is a gossip and begins to tell you about how someone did something they angrily disapprove of. Now your vibration begins to decline, and yet you didn't do anything except answer your phone to talk to this person. You were on the receiving end absorbing this negative energy your friend was outwardly darting at your soul. Now your vibration has dropped.

Some animals will dart away when they sense a hostile energy coming towards them. They're in tune with a high vibration that they guard their territory without second guessing it. However, some human souls will instead welcome the hostile energy and then become one with it. They will go along with whatever the person is complaining about to them. This drops their vibration. It's understood that you might have a complicated life and you live in ways that are not conducive to raising ones vibration. This could include living in a big city full of cold, heartless people rushing around. Know that this is all about being aware of what can and will lower your vibration, while doing your best to avoid the things you know will pull you into that state.

My spirit team says that alcohol, specifically in high amounts, lowers your vibration. This does not mean that they are pointing their finger at you demanding that you stop drinking. Your choices to do, stop, dissolve, or reduce any particular life choices that drop your vibration is for you to decide. If you enjoy drinking a bottle of wine every night and yet you regularly question why you're not content with your life, and nothing ever goes your way, then this would be one of the possibilities as to what is blocking what you desire from entering the picture. Since alcohol in high amounts blocks divine communication and lowers your vibration, then you miss out on the messages and guidance from your own spirit team that would give you the missing ingredient you crave to achieve happiness.

Some connect with their Spirit team as naturally as you brush your teeth. Others struggle to pick up on messages or they express that they're receiving nothing. Your spirit team never disappears and stops communicating with you. When you feel you are receiving nothing, then there could be a block you might be unaware of. Blocks can be something trivial such as a particular food you ingest. It can be any negative feeling you're experiencing.

You pick up on heavenly messages when your ego steps out of your higher self's way. Meditating and being in a still environment in nature is a great way to access Spirit much easier than when you're under stress or any other negative emotion. Meditating in nature raises your vibration and opens up your communication line with spirit.

Raising your vibration is a lifestyle change that needs to happen over time for your soul's benefit and not for anyone else's. There are things that need to be adopted or modified daily to reach a centered place that helps one to be more connected and at peace. In *Raising Your Vibration*, we'll look at how to identify some of the basics on what raises your vibration and what will lower it.

Chapter Two

RAISING YOUR VIBRATION
TO A HIGHER LEVEL

All human souls desire the same goal regardless of their interests, values or lifestyle choices. They want to be consistently happy more than anything in the world and to have their dreams come true. When you live in a perpetual state of unhappiness with the way things are in your life, then you reach for an addiction. This is a time waster that provides false temporary comfort. It is peculiar that you would feed your body and your soul toxic garbage. What is the point of living if you're not enjoying the moment focused and clear minded? You will justify it and make excuses for your poor choices. You will tell others, "I'm not going to be made to feel guilty. I'm just going to do it this one time." Yet, you end up doing it more than once. Before you know it, six months have passed and it's become a regular habit. When you look back on those past six months, you discover that you accomplished very little if anything at all. You are exactly in the same place that you always were. Once this truth is presented to you, then you grow negative and despondent. It feels like a heavy, weight closing in on your soul and body. To escape this nasty feeling, you reach for an addiction.

One of the reasons it is important to fine-tune your body and soul is that you open up the portal to receive Heavenly messages and guidance. You have more energy during the day to accomplish what you want, not to mention you look and feel incredible. This assists in attracting in wonderful circumstances, jobs, friendships and relationships of a higher caliber to you. This positive energy enhancement shoots outwardly into the universe brightening up the aura within and around you. This is hypnotizing and magnetic to others while becoming a recipe for tremendous situations to enter your life. When you live a joyful life, then you are more compassionate and loving to be around. People are not drawn to miserable drunks with a pessimistic attitude problem. When you take care of your body and treat your soul with the utmost respect, then the universe and Heaven returns that energy back to you tenfold. It raises your vibration closer to God. He has all of the answers you seek to navigate through what might feel like a rocky existence. Your life does not have to be treacherous, because you can experience tranquility now. Only when you have reached the place of peaceful contentment do you witness the gifts and miracles you desire.

When you grow and evolve you raise your vibration. Raising your vibration to a higher level takes work and discipline. It is adopting an entirely new way of living. It is viewing the planet, your life, your surroundings, and your soul in ways that you would not have noticed in a lower vibration state.

Some examples of necessary lifestyle changes that will raise your vibration are cleaning up your diet, eating healthier, breathing deeper, frequenting nature and partaking in regular exercise. It is also avoiding alcohol, drugs, the media, and people who are toxic, drowning in stress, depression or poor life choices. This is not to say that you should abandon family members or loved ones who are under stress. There is a fine line between getting too involved that you fall into a dark hole with them, or choosing to remain detached from their drama. You do not want to grow emotionally drawn into someone else's whirlwind of consistent upset. It does nothing to help you and nor will it help by feeding them the same vibrational words they're exuding by agreeing with their chaos. This is like sprinkling lighter fluid on a burning fire. This energy expands causing more of that same substance. It is not your place to live someone else's life for them. Saying no does not mean you are coldhearted. When you say no, you are saying yes to you.

Alcohol should be in moderation or eliminated if you have an addictive personality. I understand this being a former addict myself. Even when I was no longer addicted to drugs and alcohol, I still went through a period of what is called being a *dry addict* or *dry drunk*. This is someone who is no longer addicted or using drugs and alcohol, but is still behaving as a dysfunctional addict. The dry addict has made no positive changes within themselves and therefore is likely to go after the initial addiction again. This is not to say that angels and guides preach that you give up alcohol if you're a moderate user. They are merely saying that alcohol in regular quantities blocks the communication line with Heaven which essentially blocks awesome abundance. Choosing to reduce or eliminate alcohol is a personal choice.

For some, it's effortless to reach for an alcoholic beverage or more to decompress after a long day. This may relax you for an hour, but then as the effects of the alcohol wear off, you begin to feel lethargic, edgier and worn out. Some have pointed out the negative effects they experience as the alcohol begins to wear off. They feel gross with a heavy dense pressure that surrounds their body. An array of negative blocks is created in this process. These blocks can be dangerous as it prevents the flow of positive energy, light and manifestation to you. Alcohol has adverse health effects on your body and health in the long run. It attracts in lower energy and circumstances to your aura and soul too. It's important to avoid heavy alcohol or other negative addictions for escape as much as possible. There is no secret that regular use of large consumptions of negative vices cause future health repercussions. It also lowers your vibration and blocks the flow of positive abundance. Know that you have free will choice and that there is no judgment if you are a regular drinker. Please don't feel as if they're pointing the finger like a scolding parent. They are relaying messages to me on things that contribute to lowering your vibration. These are also things that prevent you from picking up on their messages while blocking in good stuff.

Instead of reaching for that drink, I am more inclined to exercise. I'll jog up a mountain trail, or on the beach, or anywhere in nature. It is less stressful than jogging through the busy streets. I bike regularly along the beach coast as well. Exercise centers and elevates your spirit. You have more energy in the process while appearing and feeling better too! Others notice a brighter glow around you. Your entire aura and being attracts others to you. You have more time and energy during the day to accomplish important tasks. These tasks are geared towards your life purpose, spending quality time with loved ones, and more time for healthy rest. Relaxation is a luxury as well as a necessity. Get away for a couple of days and head to a place in nature, such as a park, the desert, the mountains or the beach where it is quiet and serene. I use those surroundings as an access to re-center myself if I am feeling out of sorts. If I'm at home and unable to get away for any reason I'll put on a melodic chill out or uplifting CD album, then light some incense and candles. I will create a safe, calming sanctuary where I live.

BREATHING AND STRETCHING

Breathing is vital to your health and in raising your vibration. When you are stressed or upset, you hold your breath without realizing it. Take some time daily to sit still, pause and breathe deeply in and out. This is stopping what you are doing, taking a huge healthy breathe in for three to five seconds, and exhale out all of your worries, stresses and toxins. Imagine the pressures and tension bottled and locked up in your body and aura exiting out into the air as you exhale. Give those worries and stresses to your Spirit team and Heaven. Notice how relaxed and clear minded you begin to feel. You might experience some "lightheadness" as your body, mind and soul re-centers and re-aligns itself.

Doing this breathing exercise regularly sends and feeds oxygen to all of your organs and cells. This awakens your soul that often feels trapped and confined in its body. Those who suddenly have restless energy with an urge to take off, make drastic changes, or uproot their life in an impulsive manner feel this soul entrapment deeply. Their soul does not feel the freedom that would come naturally to them in the spirit world. Your soul suffocates in your temporary body when you feed it toxins. Your ego pushes you to make changes that will not usually bring the joy and love you crave. You might be happy once the initial change takes place, but it will not be long before you discover that you're suffocating again and the rise of restless energy is dominant. You're chasing a happiness that you will never find by running away. This is a search for something substantial that already lives within you. You need to access it and bring it out.

Taking time to partake in breathing exercises is essential to centering yourself. Yet, many human souls would rather hold their stress in. This leads to health complications by trapping in all of that unnecessary negativity and stress energy into the crevices of your body. This is an ugly breeding ground for health issues. Centering your soul helps you achieve wholeness. This adds clarity as well as a euphoric feeling of joy. It connects and merges your soul with your physical body. This helps you become aware of who you are in truth. You learn that the current functioning of human life is on the trivial side.

Incorporate body stretching into your routine. This improves your circulation and relaxes the muscles that tense up under daily stresses. Lie down on the floor and stretch every part of your body in various ways. Perhaps lay a beach towel down next to your bed and do the stretches there. If you are able to bring the towel to your backyard or a park is even better. It provides a cheering environment that ultimately relaxes you. You might not be aware that the wear and tear of your day can easily tighten up areas in your body and remain there indefinitely. All of the stresses compounded in your day become trapped into the crevices of the cells in your body. Partaking in daily breathing exercises will get a lot of that gunk out, but sometimes there are remains of it wedged into hard to reach areas that can later cause long term health issues. This also blocks the flow of good energy and vibrations throughout your body, mind and soul. This is why stretching is beneficial to your overall soul and higher self. Talking to friends who are bubbly, upbeat or positive is another way to lift your vibration. Suddenly everything shifts in and around your world. Feeling those good vibes from optimistic people, coupled with stretching and breathing exercises contributes to re-centering your being.

CUDDLING, HUGGING, TOUCHING

If you are involved with someone in a romantic relationship, then make love, and love each other up regularly. Put in frequent efforts to shower one another with supportive words. Those that are in healthy long-term, committed, love relationships are physically healthier and happier than those who are not. They are more productive and tend to live longer too. There are powerful healing benefits for couples who experience joy together and who are loyal with one another. When you are in a relationship, you need to hug one another often. This includes cuddling, making love, kissing and giving each other massages especially after long stress filled days. Do this with one another regularly no matter how ridiculous it might seem to you. If you shun or shy away from this type of physical expression, then you need to let your guard down and open your heart up to your significant other. This is important for your long-term health and your relationship! Human souls were not born closed off and unreceptive to physical expression. This is behavior that is a block grown from the outside human tampering in your life.

In this cold love relationship world, there are many human souls who are single, so these activities are not always an option. However, equally harmful is being in a relationship where there is no love showered between the couple in any form. Let your guard down and hug a friend hello when you see them. Hug an animal or a tree! This may be more of a challenge if someone is male. Men tend to reserve displays of friendly affection, but I've noticed a growing trend where the newer generations are more open to those forms of hello than the previous generations. They are a newer generation of souls who chose to enter this lifetime to spread love and joy. Love and joy are two feelings that have been lacking for centuries due to societal influences.

Sharing in the cuddling, hugging and touching activities with your mate lowers both of your cortisol levels and blood pressure. You are less stressful after a day that is compounded with negative strains. Cortisol is a stress hormone in your adrenal glands above your kidney's that shoots out to your brain when a sudden panic or attack in your life happens. This can be something as basic as feeling stressed when in traffic trying to get to work. A higher dose of this is damaging on your brain chemistry. When the nervous system is shot that high abruptly, it's not that easy for it to drop down. For some it can take as long as a day! You've likely noticed this with yourself or others who experience an alarming situation. You are also aware with how long throughout the day you or this person carried that alarm state within. This is what this cortisol hormone is. It can cause adrenal fatigue as you may have experienced following a stress filled situation. Hours after the stress event, you feel worn out. Some might cry out, "I cannot wait to have a drink!" Adrenal fatigue is also when you receive the recommended seven to eight hours of sleep a night, yet you feel tired and sluggish all day.

If you find that you are always tired no matter how much sleep you get, then there are an abundant amount of possibilities of what could be causing that. It can be that you are unhappy in any area of your life. Maybe it's your job, relationship or home life. When you are experiencing daily doom and gloom feelings due to one or more of these areas, this drains you of life force and vitality! Just one of these areas can leave you perpetually tired. This tiredness is disguising a form of depression. If there is more than one area of your life that brings you down, then double or triple the energy of this feeling to understand the impact. Overtime this will take its toll on your body, mind and soul. Naturally, the most obvious thing to do is get a physical with a doctor to rule out any potential health issues outside of being unhappy with life. Once that's ruled out, then the answer is in front of you. It is poor diet, not enough exercise, or dissatisfaction in one or more areas of your life. Identify where the root cause of this tiredness is coming from. Get happy now by making positive adjustments with the areas in your life that cause you daily grief. Doing this in steps won't make it feel so overwhelming.

Cuddling, hugging and touching have immense healing properties as discussed. These acts are able to bring down your cortisol levels more rapidly than anything else. When you engage in these activities with someone, or your romantic partner, it will assist in lightening the load of unhappiness in your life. It will raise your vibration and boost your Oxytocin levels. Oxytocin is known as the love hormone. This calms your entire body and helps your soul brighten and shine. It blasts away any potential health problems. This will also open up your clair channels to receive clear accurate messages and guidance from Heaven. The guidance you receive is transparent while in this state. It contains the answer to your prayer that pulls you out of the darkness you were previously experiencing.

Touching relaxes you and lowers your blood pressure. Hold hands and touch your partner often. When you touch your partner, it merges your souls with one another. There is the emotional impact that reassures you both that you are protected and comfortable. This elevates both of your vibrations to a place of contentment and satisfaction. Touching has great benefits for the physical and metaphysical heart. Shaking someone's hand in a warm and friendly manner merges your energies, brightening up both of your auras if even for an hour.

There isn't enough reaching out and expressions of love in this world to begin with. When someone is exuding negative traits and directing them outwardly towards anyone in their way, they are masking an inner despair. Grab them and hug them up to melt those wasted toxic feelings that do not help them or anybody around. Can you imagine that instead of war you hugged your enemies? The vibration of this entire planet would rise to a phenomenal degree. It would create a beautiful, loving place where all human souls live in harmony and joy indefinitely.

EMOTIONAL EATING

Health and diet are crucial areas of focus that need to be adhered to in order to raise your vibration. You were not meant to consume chips and hot dogs on a regular basis! You were not meant to cause harm and destruction to your body, emotional state and each other. There was once a time in history when humankind was living to be hundreds of years old. The food that existed then was what you were intended to consume. Eventually food grew to be complex and interesting. It would be injected with hormones and chemicals. Now you are fed a poisonous diet of processed foods and fats. America alone prides itself on the fast food diet. This is what some people raise their children on because it's fast and cheap. This is simultaneously programming the upcoming generations to become addicted to food that is lethal to your body. In a strange way, they are preparing you to die early by slowly poisoning you with bad foods. You become addicted to certain deadly foods and carry that with you throughout your life. Eating this way lowers your vibration, weighs your soul down, and causes a dark array of future health issues. Some of the highest obesity rates exist in the world today. Even if someone is not obese, they are living off food filled with lard, saturated fats and cholesterol. Only select groups read the ingredient labels on the back of food packaging, and understand what they're truly putting in their body. These foods are made with an abundant amount of ingredients that contain words that most people cannot pronounce. These words are all different names for sugar, food coloring and chemicals. It's like pouring water into your car gas tank and attempting to drive. This is essentially what is being put into your body. It's another disguise for controlling the masses. They have everyone move around dangerously pumped up on chemicals. This causes them to function severely sluggish or under stress.

The mantra that says you must do everything in moderation is important, however, eliminating negative substances altogether is even better. Unfortunately, human ego gets in the way convincing you that you need that piece of chocolate cake! The bad foods and drinks that you consume are emotional eating and a result of something bigger going on underneath.

There is an underlying emptiness and cause going on within you that prompts you to have repeated cravings for something like Pizza or Ice Cream. God, the angels and spirits in Heaven do not say any of this to ensure you feel miserable. It may seem like that when they urge you to clean up your diet and avoid bad foods, soda, alcohol or drugs. On the contrary, by cleaning up your diet you grow to become more focused and happier in the long run. You experience longer lasting feelings of pleasure and enjoyment, rather than feeling blocked and weighed down by sugar or alcohol. You attract in at higher positive levels while awakening your spiritual connection line to Heaven. You are more readily able to hear, see, feel and know the messages and guidance that your own Spirit team wishes to relay to you that can assist you on a joyful path. If you do not make these changes and life modifications, then you are likely to stay in the same place you have been in your life to date.

HARSH ENERGIES

The energies around the world are harsh everyday and that is just the sad reality now. Despite this, everything is slowly shifting in a more positive way thanks to the many evolved souls who have incarnated from the Realms and Spirit Worlds that exist. With those shifts comes the tantrum throwing by lower evolved human souls. This is what you are bearing witness to around the world. Before the harsh energies came at you once in awhile, but now it is out of control and happens on a daily basis. The internet, technology and phone apps that exist have positive uses, but most do not use it for positive purposes. Technological devices spit out toxic energy at your aura and latches onto your soul. If one is using the devices for selfish reasons, such as to spew negativity, or for ego stroking, then you and the person they direct the energy to will be a magnet for some of these harsh energies.

Do not continue down the path of living in turmoil. This causes you to display agitating energies that the Universe rejects entirely. When this happens, you are denied great abundance and instead find the agitating energies to be mirrored and reflected right back to you.

It is important to make certain lifestyle changes that include avoiding harsh situations and people as much as possible. Steer your soul away from all drama that exists. It is all "noise", which is energy that you do not want to be a part of. There is no love or benefit that exists in that area.

Due to the energy being intense on Earth, you need to ensure you keep your life balanced in all areas that exist, such as your personal and professional life. Your life is balanced when both areas have equal attention. Unfortunately, most human souls work more than they play and relax. This is discussed to some degree in the part two of this book, *Empowering Spirit Wisdom*. Balancing your internal energies can be done by taking quiet retreats or spending quality time alone. Get away for a couple of days to do nothing, but relax and enjoy yourself. You do not have to go away out of town if you do not have the money or time. You can go to a park and unwind for fifteen to thirty minutes. What happens when you are alone in nature amidst trees, grass, plants and flowers? You feel a relaxing calming effect on your aura. I've walked through gorgeous parks to see people alone sitting near trees with a half smile on their faces content with the energy that is overcoming them. You certainly do not relax sitting in your car in traffic, or trying to cross a busy street with horns honking, and people shooting harsh invisible daggers carelessly in the air.

There is great emphasis for you to take these nature retreats. You need regular stretches of time off. Get away from the noise and balance the energies in your often stress filled life. This gives you the opportunity to clear your mind of all that debris that latches onto your aura with its claws. Ask your Spirit team to help by giving you the time and resources to incorporate regular retreats and time outs. You can ask them mentally, in a prayer, or out loud, and even in writing.

EXERCISE AND FITNESS

The Earth's atmosphere is extremely heavy and compressed. This adds additional blocks that can make it difficult for many to connect to the Spirit world, even though your Spirit team connects with you on a daily basis. The stuff you put into your body contributes to these blocks including things such as cigarettes, alcohol, drugs, violence, anger, revenge and dysfunctional relationships. Negativity and gossip as well as poor diets and lack of exercise are other factors. This is why it is demanded that you take care of your body and be mindful of your life choices and habits.

I'm a strong advocate for health and fitness no matter what age someone is. Since I was a child, my Guides and Angels have been sharing with me that exercising and taking care of ourselves physically is our #1 obligation to do while here. You have to take care of your body! It is a gift enabling you to function and accomplish your goals and manifestations while you are living here. You have to care about it and your soul.

Heaven considers certain things a sin, although the word sin isn't in their vocabulary, but the meaning is still the same. One of those sins is: Lack of Exercise. You are urged to take care of your body. You must take the vessel you are living in with incredible seriousness.

Some souls have elected to come into this lifetime where physical exercise may be impossible. Know that when they say exercise and take care of your body, this is to do it in the best possible way that you are able to. Not everyone can run up a mountain, but there are light cardio exercises one can do. There are stretches one can do or lighter forms of exercise movement. There is a difference between whining that you don't feel like it, or that you have other things to do and are too tired, or that you physically cannot do it due to a life health circumstance that prevents it.

Before computers, cell phones and even television sets, how did humankind get through the day? They spent more time outdoors! The bigger cities were not as busy and congested as they are now. You could go for peaceful walks right in the middle of the largest city. Now thanks to the greed in human ego, this spawned an indefinite need to over develop where nature once existed. This self-indulgence produced the over population of humankind on planet Earth. You have to search for a nature preserve or a park unless you live in such a location. Before the days of electricity, light or clocks for that matter, people did not obsess over the distractions that exist today. We would be outdoors and head to bed when the sun went down. The next morning, there was a full day packed with more energy to accomplish what is needed. The enhanced physical energy was due to having a full night's sleep and being outdoors partaking in physical activity. The foods were not full of chemicals and toxins in the way that they are now.

If I am on a large amount of caffeine, then hearing my own Guides and Angels is difficult. As a Clairaudient, it is as if the sound has been turned down low. Caffeine speeds up your heart and therefore your anxiety levels. Anxiety and stress block heavenly communication. In order to turn up the volume of your Guides and Angels, remove negative substances such as coffee, sodas and other heavily caffeinated drinks. Are you addicted to energy drinks? They tend to be consumed mostly by teenagers, young college adults and busy professionals. Imagine the toll this has on your heart over time. Pouring sugar, chemicals and way too much caffeine into your system on a regular basis like that is a bomb waiting to go off. I have been guilty of consuming energy drinks in abundance. At one point in my life, I was doing it daily without a care in the world. I would say, "Oh there's a ton of B vitamins in this." Yeah, and add to that the list of sugars, caffeine in large amounts, and other chemicals no one can pronounce.

Many of the toxins I mention, I have been guilty of consuming like a fiend at one time or another. It was only after my Spirit team consistently warned me about the repercussions did I realize that I had to work on making healthy life changes. Take caution and pay attention to the consumption of toxins you ingest on a regular basis. Aim for dissolving or reducing these harmful products when possible.

Your body is an instrument designed to receive messages from God when you are operating at a higher frequency. You are unable to do that efficiently when you are consuming high amounts of caffeine or alcohol. Heavy stints of caffeine increase anxiety and hypertension, which can cause long-term health problems as well. When I'm doing something that will affect me negatively, my left ear rings loudly at times. This is my Spirit team's way of getting my attention and downloading information to assist me in dissolving my cravings for these more dangerous, addictive, substance behaviors.

Water is also a critical necessity you need to consume lots of. Your body is compiled of water. God created tons of water in and all around human souls for a reason. This is to ensure that you keep your body in operable condition while you are using it. One of the ways this is accomplished is by drinking water. This hydrates and fuels all of your organs flushing out all of the toxins you breathe into your body. These pollutants and waste stay in your body causing damage to your kidneys if they are not rinsed out repeatedly with water. When you drink plenty of water you have more energy, a clearer complexion, and not to mention you look better too! I have been drinking over eight glasses of water since I was a teenager. I carry a huge missile of water with me every day and have been doing that since I was seventeen. One of my many secrets is having a disciplined exercise regimen that includes consuming at least eight glasses of water a day. Your water consumption needs to be done indefinitely.

Exercise is significant in maintaining your body, mind and soul. You do not need to be a hardcore body builder or world-renowned athlete. My Spirit team has explained to me that some body building lifestyles fall surprisingly into the realm of addictions. These people pump themselves up daily with chemicals before they spend hours working on their body. Some of them view their bodies with a distorted view not realizing when they are doing too much. You may have likely heard of cases where prime athletic and fit people have had a sudden heart attack. This isn't because they were fit and athletic of course. The cause was all of the harsh chemicals they ingest on a regular basis to pump them up to exercise. This sounds much like a catch 22. You're feeding yourself these chemicals in order to take care of your body. Doing this on a daily basis can actually cause the opposite effect such as heart failure or other health complications.

The other form of exercise addiction is when you work out purely for vanity reasons. Your frame of mind is in the wrong place causing an unhealthy obsession connected to body image. This lowers your vibration.

I enjoy cardio more than several times a week. I head to the gym to use the weight machines or the free weights at home on a weekly basis. I will randomly drop down to do pushups. I am always active and keeping my body as healthy as I can. Exercising and being active has always been like oxygen to me. There are days where my energy level is low, but I push myself to get started with some cardio if even for a short bit. About five to ten minutes of jogging and your blood starts pumping through your organs. Exercise fights feelings of anxiety and depression prompting you to be more alert and energetic. It also releases endorphins, which make one happy giving them uplifting feelings.

When you head for a jog, start out by walking briskly for about three to five minutes to get your joints lubricated, and then move into your jog. If it's a short jog, then after about another fifteen minutes give yourself an additional five minutes to cool down at the end. Avoid stopping abruptly and sitting down immediately. This is not good on your heart. You'll want to have a cool down process where the jog slows down into a walk for a few minutes. There are lighter forms of exercise you may find more suitable for your sensibilities and body chemistry such as Yoga, Pilates or Tai Chi. Do anything besides sitting on the couch all day, in your car, or in an office chair. Get at least fifteen minutes of brisk exercise everyday. Do it several times a day if you are able to. Get moving!

I carry my gym bag everywhere for those days where I know I will not be back home for awhile. If you head straight home before you go to the gym, you might talk yourself out of going. When you arrive at home, you are comfortable and just want to relax. Stopping at the gym on the way home has many benefits like giving you a break from rush hour traffic!

Chapter Three

REMOVING ADDICTIONS AND NEGATIVE SUBSTANCES

*O*t was not easy or immediate when I was brought to a permanent healthier space in my life. I was a compulsive addict as I discuss in my book, *Reaching for the Warrior Within.* I was addicted to drugs, alcohol, over the counter prescription medications, cigarettes, coffee, sugar and even dysfunctional relationships and people! One by one, my Spirit team started dissolving or reducing my cravings for those addictions. I did not go through any professional therapy. I accomplished this with the power of my mind and the help of my Spirit team. I was surprised to find that I was happier and more energetic when not using any of those vices.

Coffee blocks and dims the communication

waves to Heaven. My Spirit team said I didn't need it. Naturally, I argued as I do with anyone who is pushing me to do something I disagree with. I was not a big coffee drinker to begin with, but I did have one cup of coffee every morning. The rest of the day I would be drinking a huge bottle of water. I fought with my Spirit team on this. Others were far more into their coffee than I was, and those people were drinking tons of it. Researchers have said that one-cup a day has shown no negative adverse health effects. I always showed up to battle or to debate by having done my research.

Every morning I would get up at 7:30am tired, even after sleeping my mandatory minimum eight hours a night. I would head over to my fancy French press to make that perfect cup of coffee. As I was getting ready, I'd continuously hear my Spirit team say, *"You don't need it."* I'd ignore them and grumble. "Yes I do." I would need concrete proof that I don't need it in order for me to quit.

One day after the nudges persisted, I slammed my hands down and said, "Okay if you don't believe I need coffee and I think I do, then I give you full permission to assist me in reducing my cravings for it. That's the only way I see this working. If I'm craving coffee, then there's no stopping me. I'm going to have it, unless you can help me with this then too."

They agreed in succession.

The next morning I woke up feeling unusually alive as I went into the kitchen. I thought, "Hmm, I'm not craving any coffee this morning. That's odd. I might try and do without it today. Let's test this out."

About one month later, I discovered I was having one cup of coffee a few times a week instead of every single morning. Over the course of the months that followed, it was one cup of coffee once or twice a week. This moved into once or twice every couple of weeks. This pattern continued until by month six, I was no longer drinking coffee at all! After twenty years of drinking a cup every morning I no longer craved coffee. I discovered I had more energy and less stress. I have the coffee bag in my house, but the same bag has been sitting there unused for emergencies or guests. I haven't found the need for an emergency. Even if I did, I would not beat myself up over it. You take it one day at a time. Do the best you can as you dissolve unhealthy substances gradually and safely. The way they removed coffee was the same way they removed cigarettes, hard drugs and heavy drinking. They were all gone just like that. No urge. No craving. It was miraculous as the change happened after I made my official request to my Guides and Angels for assistance.

The world spends billions of dollars on coffee daily. Some buy that fancy cup of coffee every day at whatever coffee franchise is on the way to their work. Imagine spending about $3.00-$4.00 a day five days a week. You're spending $80.00 a month on a coffee drink that has no benefit to your health or bank account. Other than waking you up for a couple of hours, it exasperates your stress and anxiety levels throughout the rest of the day. Please know that it is not advocated that you stop drinking coffee. This is a personal choice that you decide on with your Spirit team. There is no judgment if you enjoy your coffee. They're merely stating the repercussions and negative side effects that lower your vibration and block or dim heavenly communication.

There are parents who pump their kids up daily with caffeinated sodas giving them repeated injections of caffeine and sugar. This is what you do with the soul you allegedly love? Granted it's not done with malice, but out of naivety and society's influence. I was one of those kids who would revel in the occasional soda. Luckily, my taste for dangerous foods and drinks were in adolescence. Even while consuming this stuff, I was "claircognizantly" aware that this was not good for the body. You have one body and you have to take care of it. You have to care about it and yourself. I do not have a sweet tooth or have a craving for desserts. I can walk past a buffet table spread to the gills with cakes, cookies, ice cream and yet there is no temptation.

The painful issues you focus on are self-induced by yourself, your ego, and those you surround yourself with. You can eliminate the pain and issues as I did with the assistance of your own team of Guides and Angels. You do need to formally request their help since they cannot intervene with your free will. They can only intervene when you make a request. Ask God, or whoever you equate God to be, to send you a health and lifestyle angel or guide. This is one that will work with you daily on making the shift into a stronger self. After your request, you will need to pay attention to the signs and messages around you. They will place these signs around you, or nudge you to make positive adjustments in your life. For example, they may guide you to a certain gym class by consistently dropping the flyer to this class in your path repeatedly until you finally take notice that it is divinely orchestrated.

My Spirit team worked with me to change my life one-step at a time. I have never felt as great as I do today. I had more energy, stamina and optimism at thirty-five than I did at twenty-five. I was more physically fit at thirty-five than I was at twenty-five, which means you can do it too!

Instead of coffee, I juice one cucumber in the morning with a juicer machine. I might add anything from Maca powder or parsley. Sometimes if I want a real kick, I'll juice a clove of garlic with it and add a splash of Cayenne pepper spice. This healthy alternative gives me just what I need and in better ways than a measly cup of coffee that would only exasperate my stress, anxiety and depression. I would later crash from the coffee, but the cucumber juice keeps on going. My mind is clearer and the messages from Spirit are opened up wider. Before this change, the messages were dim and faint. Cucumber juice is also great for your complexion. It cleans and clears out the toxins built up in your organs. It's fantastic on your lymphatic system and far less costly than paying for a daily cup of coffee.

In those days when I was guided to eliminate

coffee, my Guides and Angels nudged me to reduce and eliminate sugar. Granted, I would sprinkle a little bit of sugar in coffee, tea or cereal to begin with, but did I really need it? I wanted to test it out and see if I could do without it. I stopped sprinkling granulated sugar on anything after that and never went back. Instead, I use a healthier alternative such as a spice like cinnamon or nutmeg. Coincidentally nutmeg has its own healing properties. It is great as a brain stimulant and relieves stress and depression among other things. Cinnamon is high in nutrients and lowers cholesterol. Both are a much healthier alternative to sugar, which has zero benefits and is toxic to your body and health. I was surprised by how much I loved the taste of cinnamon after that. It far exceeds that of granulated sugar. The same goes for salt. I never used salt in all of my life, but the rare occasions where salt is needed for myself or a friend, I offer Sea Salt or Himalayan Salt, which is not damaging to your body the way processed salt is. In fact, it detoxifies and assists in balancing the energies and cells in your body.

When I quit cigarettes at age twenty-five, I had a box hidden away in case of an emergency, even though that day never came. It is preferred that you throw away whatever it is you're trying to quit. The reason is you have some of that energy hanging around the house. There is no temptation if the product is not there. I later stumbled upon the cigarettes in a box and ended up throwing it away realizing I was no longer a smoker. I never had any cravings for cigarettes after the age of twenty-five.

Ironically, I'm unable to stand immediately next to someone who is smoking around me. Friends that are the occasional smoker will not smoke around me or they will disappear somewhere outside down the street away from my vicinity. It's not polite to force others to breathe in the air of cigarette smoke. Even when I was a smoker in the early days, it was rare that I was seen smoking. I never did it around a non-smoker out of respect. Whereas hardcore smokers would run through a pack a day, it would take me several weeks to a month before my pack would run out. I was a casual smoker, but have been cigarette free since 1999. It's hard to believe I smoked at this point since I demand fresh breathable air around me. I found it easier to walk past a window with marijuana smoke wafting out into my lunges, than cigarette smoke.

As a former addict, I can tell you that most of the people using drugs, alcohol or any other toxic vice are running from something that includes some form of emotional or mental trauma. There are human souls who use these vices because they enjoy the way it makes them feel. If they enjoy the way it makes them feel, it's because they don't like how they feel when they're not on anything. Why don't you like how you feel without being on anything? The inadequacy inside you is a false reality. Everyone is too busy fixing their outsides so people will find them attractive or like them, but they are not bothering to correct the core problem, which lies inside you. You are more attractive when you exude that from the inside out.

Ask your own Guides and Angels to steer you

towards a healthier lifestyle. All you have to do is say the words, *"Please help me with...."* And then pay attention to the signs and messages that they put in your path.

They also assisted me in removing my need or hankerings for anti-depressant and anxiety medication. I started using it after one of my relationship break ups, and then ended up staying on it for three years. It was not easy waning off the drug as I had become dependent on it. I attempted to dissolve the medication through repeated attempts on my own with no success. Another relationship ended in the process as I was attempting to wane off it again. At that point I said, "Oh forget it, I need to stay on this a little while longer." I also discovered the anti-depressants helped me with my social anxiety. I did not want to be on it forever and preferred to function as clear minded as I possibly could.

I asked my Spirit team and Archangel Raphael to help me find healthy alternatives that are superior for my body, mind and soul. Nothing was going to stop me from dissolving it. They guided me to the right vitamins that were deficient in me. This isn't to say that everyone should dissolve their anti-depressant medication. This was a personal choice that I wanted to do. You should always discuss dissolving your prescribed medication with your Doctor first. I know what it's like to struggle with lifelong anxiety and depression symptoms.

I was determined to live as naturally as I could while trusting that I would be okay. I was on the anti-depressant drug Effexor for several years.

After I asked for heavenly assistance, they guided me to a reduced anti-depressant in Wellbutrin. They do not abruptly take you off something, but instead gradually wane and reduce you off of your addiction much like a Doctor would. After six months of the Wellbutrin, I took the last tablet in the pack. I agreed with my Spirit team, that I would take it day to day from that point. Granted I was slightly nervous over how long I could go before I faltered. I would not push myself any further that I didn't think I could do. In the end, I haven't had a prescribed anti-depressant medication tablet since that day.

It is more than cutting all of these toxic consumptions out, but I personally had to cut many things out of my life as I shifted into becoming a Warrior of Light. This included the biggest culprits and cause of my addictions: Certain people. Toxic, negative and abusive people were all out and gone! Those around you contribute to one succumbing to a pill or vice to begin with. The insufficient and uncomfortable feelings that lead you to the drug were not there when you were born. I had joked with a friend once that people are on medication…because of other people! It's others that should be on medication. Don't give them that power. Tell them no, go away and get lost. It was Archangel Raphael that helped me off anti-depressants without any support from anyone around me. He altered my entire life into something positive. He cleared the debris and toxins from within and around my body.

CLEAR THE CLUTTER

Simplify your life by eliminating the clutter in and around you. This will help bring any hidden positive energy out and moving. You accumulate clutter everyday from material things to other people's energies. The angels have shown me that this clutter is similar to a drainpipe in a sink. When hair and gunk gets stuck in those pipes the water doesn't flow freely. This same concept goes for your bodies and the life around you. It blocks good things from flowing easily to and from you. This includes good energy streaming through the organs and cells in your body and soul.

You do not realize how stagnant the energy in your life is when stuck in a rutted routine. Educating yourself and becoming a lifelong student of higher learning is another additional way to raise your vibration. Your diet and what you consume has an effect on your overall well-being and energy level. High vibrational foods are fruits and vegetables, especially organic foods which are free of pesticides. Avoid sugar and alcohol, along with foods and substances filled with preservatives. Drugs are a definite no, as it has detrimental effects on your vibration, health and the relationships around you. It blocks messages from Heaven while opening up the portal for negative energies to attach themselves to you. You'll know this has happened to you when your life spirals out of control. You might experience one poor circumstance after another or feel eternally lethargic and moody.

I have seen many rave about soy products, which does have positive benefits, specifically the whole fermented soy. Then you have the other soy products that exist such as, Soy Lecithin, Soy Protein Concentrate and Isolate to name a few. These are all names for chemical preservatives. It's appalling to know how much food is manufactured and eaten that contain harmful forms of soy. Human souls are more or less being slowly poisoned by the masses.

Men should avoid soy or reduce it when possible. This may seem impractical considering that the food industries have chosen to infuse some form of soy in their products. Soy increases estrogen levels in men. The nutrition and diet industries have been feeding the health benefits of soy to the public, but the problem is they are not mentioning the repercussions on men specifically. Kids have been raised on soy more than ever before. The boys will hit a hormone drop in their mid-thirties instead of the expected mid-forties because of this. Soy suppresses a man's sex drive because of the immediate drop in testosterone along with other side effects.

Besides waking up the next day with a hangover from alcohol or drugs, do you ever notice that it takes a great deal of effort to get yourself and your body back up to standard? It takes longer than a day to get there and some don't even survive the week without consuming another drink or drug. The older you get, the harder it is on your body, which is why many quit altogether. If they don't, then their poor bodies just give out and stop working resulting in death. They exit this life long before their time.

Retreat often and take vacations to decompress the built up stresses you've added onto your soul. A time out is necessary even if you don't have enough time. Make the time! Eliminate people from your life that drain and suck your high energy dry. Abolish those that consistently lead you to partake in activities that are not healthy for your soul and body.

I've always been a firm believer that having a drink or some bad food in moderation is okay. Moderation means once in a blue moon. Yet, many souls slip out of that moderation and it ends up becoming a regular habit.

You are here to fulfill your life purpose, learn soul enhancing lessons, gain knowledge, and to enjoy this life and have some fun. This fun does not fall into the category of toxic. You are not asked to stop these poor ways of living for anyone's benefit, but your own. Heaven wants you to live at your fullest potential while experiencing euphoric feelings of joy. When you participate in healthy activities, exercise regularly, and have some measure of discipline about what you put into your body, then the fun and enjoyment you experience is beyond cosmic. If a stressful situation hits you, then as a high vibration soul you are able to take on that stress in exhilarating stride. You are equipped to allowing the stress to roll off you without tampering with your energy field. The stressed situation evaporates rather quickly, than it would if you had not asked your Spirit team to intervene and work with you.

Your individual blocks need to be identified through personal self-analysis. You can do this by being as truthful with yourself as possible in order to extricate those blocks out of your life. Be objective during this process and get your ego out of the way. Blocks are what prevent you from achieving happiness and your wildest dreams of abundance from Heaven.

AVOID GOSSIP

I don't watch regular television and nor do I have it hooked up. I do watch movies on DVD though. I stay away from the news because it's mostly always spun in a negative way to get everyone riled up or to bring them down. It also prompts others to gossip and argue their beliefs and opinions back and forth. This does nothing to help them, the other person, or the situation they are arguing about. Yet, it is impossible not to notice the headlines at times when you are checking your email for example. When you read the negative headlines, or absorb that energy, then you have invited it into your vicinity to hang out. It tampers with your aura and darkens your energy. Your self-esteem plummets and your soul grows dark and muddy. It also blocks Heaven's wonders from entering into your life. Once you plunge into the dark depths of the abyss, it is difficult to climb back out of it.

Work on reversing any negative effects built up by being considerate and thoughtful with your media and lifestyle choices. Be mindful of how you communicate with others and who you allow into your world. When you express compassion towards someone else, the energy lifts you and the other person as well. You are no longer burdened by the weight of that darkness. Allowing yourself to be affected by someone else in a negative way erodes your self-esteem. Your energy and state of mind becomes messy and full of confusion. You grow agitated and feelings of low self worth permeate through your body. Do not fight against the current by being affected by those around you. Recognize this when it happens and start treating yourself a bit better. Do not worry about the news headlines or what others are saying. All of that is noise that does nothing to bring people together. Give yourself a time frame such as a week where you avoid the news and gossip. Notice if it lifts your state of mind into optimism. You might find that your life is indeed in a more peaceful space than it was before. Optimism is a powerful attracter of your Universal desires.

Remain Optimistic

Millions of people around the world acknowledge holidays, their birthdays, or even the end of the year as a guide to see how far they have improved or progressed. They look at it as a time out to celebrate with optimism in hopes that the future will be brighter for them. It is when people will often say, "Next year will be better." If you keep saying tomorrow will be better, then you will always be one step away from happiness. Feel peacefulness today and then your challenges will lessen.

You are being asked to examine your life in a deeper way in order to make significant positive changes. Many human souls have been waking up in the process. This transformation you have been going through will make someone's ego unhappy, because change is something different than what you are accustomed to. You get uncomfortable whenever there is a drastic adjustment that forces you out of your comfort zone.

There is often fear energy talk surrounding new diseases or an end of the world. These are all false fads that are beat upon society by human ego. There is never going to be an end of the world, but the negativity and the obsessive focus on that sort of talk amplifies the darker sides of the world's character.

Get unstuck so you can be at a place that benefits your soul. Evaluate your beliefs, values and ways of doing things and make significant changes in your life immediately. Shed all of that garbage from in and around you. This will open you up to be receptive to the wonderful circumstances headed your way. Be open to receive those gifts in the right spirit and start living fully today.

Awaken Your Inner Child Through Joy

Inviting laughter into your life is crucial to your well-being. It opens up your heart while awakening and unleashing your inner child. It has profound health benefits next to love. Love and joy are two of the highest energy vibrations in the universe. The entire Spirit world is bathed in the wonders of exuding those powerful feelings eternally. These are some of the biggest most recurring messages I receive. The messages they give me are sometimes repetitive if they are not being followed. The messages sound easy enough, but why is it so hard for some souls to live in that space 24/7?

Many lives are full of stresses, toxins and disappointments. You have no problem living in those conditions and choosing grief instead of harmony. This way of living is thrust upon you by others. It is a learned trait because you certainly were not born that way. You come into contact with someone who is negative or toxic and you absorb that energy. You end up taking it out on someone else and they pay that forward and so forth. Your aura and soul darkens along with your state of mind. Soon you are behaving like that too. You pass it around to one another like contagion. This is what gets passed around when it should be lightheartedness, optimism, love and laughter. Many choose a path of deep anguish where they allow that distress to drop to a level where no one can reach them.

I sense every range of energy in the air without escape and we are indeed stressed globally. There are evolved souls in this lifetime spreading humor and joy, but it's not enough to get the tides moving fast enough. Get everyone to join in!

It can be challenging being around others who are permanently mired in negativity and you cannot get away from them. They may be a romantic partner, family member, roommates and the worst offenders, which are colleagues. The reason they are the worst offenders is because many human souls spend most of their days with those they work with. You cannot escape them. If that one draining apple exists in the bunch, they have the power to shift the entire mood within the work environment. Typically that one sour grape is keen on spreading it around to others who are not interested. This causes a decline in productivity and morale. It takes great effort to raise it again. This is carried over into your daily personal life when you head outside, brave the streets, and eventually head home. You pass that energy to your friends and loved ones. You suppress it or feed it by getting your hands on a toxic addiction.

A friend sent me one of those social media tests that allow you to check to see what your mental age is. I scored the lowest in our group showing that my mental age is nineteen. I joked that I am either immature or young at heart. This is an example of keeping your responsibilities and commitments balanced, but also remaining young at heart. Take some time out daily to see the humor in life. Make light of situations that would otherwise be distressing. You might have put your body into a tense position, or perhaps you are stuck in a rut without realizing it. You can get unstuck if you remember to have fun and unleash your inner child. You remember that kid when it was little. You saw the wonder and joy in the smallest things. When you laugh and have fun it opens up your heart Chakra, which not only invites romantic and loving situations into your life, but enables you to manifest your glorious dreams.

DANCING AND SINGING

Dancing raises your vibration! So get up, move and hit the dance floor! This is a quick way to awaken all of your cells at once. Dancing prompts you to feel alive. It opens your aura and soul right up. Your inner light blasts wide open and radiates when you dance. It does not matter where you do it. Take some time to crank up your stereo at home. Dance in your living room or in your bedroom. Sway your body and get into it. Do not feel ashamed. The spirit world is bathed in the fun of singing and dancing for a reason. They do not place the kinds of shameful or embarrassing burdens on their backs the way a human soul's ego might.

When you dance you experience joy, gratitude and optimism. Some of our greatest entertainers throughout the world's history whose specialties have been dancing on stage or screen agreed to a human life to bring this wonder to the masses all at once. Their goal is and has been to liven up human souls who get stuck in the mundane unable to break loose. It took a long time for human souls to become aware of the joys of singing and dancing. The spirit world agreed to send souls to enter into human form and display what they have been doing on all spirit planes for eons. And that is dancing and singing! Your thoughts and feelings are uplifted when you dance. Who cares if you feel you have two left feet and are tone deaf. To God, you are perfect in every way, so do it anyway! This is for your own long-term health benefit.

Society has established so many ridiculous rules that hold human souls captive. This includes restricting each other from opening up and releasing. There was once a bigger stigma with dancing when it came to men specifically. Men were trained by society to remain withdrawn, the rock, unemotional, yet strong. Men were trained to not display emotion or feelings, let alone dance. To do so would make you weak. It's the opposite in fact. It takes strength to reveal feelings and emotion. Expressing yourself through dancing and singing releases your soul from the trappings of human life!

Statistics have shown that women live longer than men. Why do you think that is? For one, women tend to be more expressive with their emotions and feelings. They do not typically hold this stuff in. They are receptive and nurturing by nature. However, a shift has taken place over the last few decades where the life expectancy for both men and women are relatively similar. This is due to men being taught to be more open, feeling oriented and expressive. They get out there on the dance floor and do not care what others think. They're not afraid to move to the music. In fact, even though there are still some traces of stigma in certain areas around the world with dancing, the newer souls coming into this world now are defying those absurd stereotypes that once held the human soul prisoner. European cultures such as Italy or Spain tend to radiate their love for dancing and expressing joy full time. Other cultures are slowly moving in that direction in a bigger way. Let's crack it wide open!

Dancing and singing releases those rigid blocks that later cause health concerns. You live a longer more prosperous life when you get into the groove.

One interesting dichotomy my Spirit team has shown me is that some partake in drugs or drinking tons of alcohol and then they get out on the dance floor. The reason this is contradictory is that even though they are at the clubs or a party dancing which raises their vibration, the alcohol and drugs soon drop your vibration to a great degree. It's counterproductive where your vibration is not rising at all.

There is nothing wrong with alcohol in moderation or that it is kept to a healthy minimum of two glasses, but the dancing and singing they're talking about is the natural kind when you're not on any mind altering substances. The dancing and singing is what will raise your vibration and overall view naturally without the need for a toxic substance. Alcohol releases inhibitions, but a human soul with a high vibration releases these inhibitions naturally without any harmful vices. Crank up your stereo or music player and move that body! Not only does your vibration rise, but these movements tone and strengthen your body with regular bouts of dancing exercise. Dancing and singing raises your vibration and releases your higher soul from its body confinement. This prompts your entire aura to feel alive!

Chapter Four

PURIFICATION KEEPS
YOUR WORLD CLEAR

$\mathcal{A}$s you make positive life changes and adjustments that include modifications to your diet and your exercise routines, it is vital to be aware when antagonistic energies are in your vicinity. Most human souls head to work on a daily basis only to be met with a colorful array of personalities. Some are good and some are shooting invisible daggers at you. If clairvoyance is your opened *clair* channel, then you may see this energy. If you are clairsentient, then you are feeling what others are pouring into you as if you are a drainpipe for their pollutants.

There are techniques you can partake in that can minimize or eliminate the effects the damage causes you at the hands of others. You will need to keep an open mind about some of these methods described in this chapter. Have trust and faith it is real. These methods do and have worked for me and countless others. You need to be disciplined about it. You can always test my Guides and Angels hypothesis before you discredit it. Hearing my Spirit team repeatedly instruct me to do these things, I folded and decided to try it out. Granted at first I was grumbling as I was doing it: "This is ridiculous." It wasn't long before I noticed the positive changes and improvements in my life.

CORD CUTTING

It can be challenging making the transition into a worker and warrior of light. Sometimes there are people in your life who hold you back from evolving. They get in the way, have zero support or cause you grief. If there are certain people you wish would go away, then you can do so by what is called *cutting cords* or *cord cutting*. It is almost like magic in the way it astonishingly works. With some suspects, it can take awhile to remove them out of your life, but you need to cut cords to them every single day. Do not give up or stop cutting cords until you feel the circumstance has improved. I have witnessed incredible results over the course of my life doing this for myself or I would not continue with it.

Anytime you connect and form a relationship with or to someone whether that is a family member, friend, colleague, business or love relationship, you form an etheric cord of attachment to them. Clairvoyantly this looks like an etheric gasoline hose coming out of the other person and hooking itself onto you. If the person is needy, negative, or always stressed for example, they are pulling high vibrational energy out of your soul. This feels as if someone is sucking the life force right out of you. This gasoline hose is really a dark etheric cord that clairvoyantly looks like spider webs wrapped around this tube strangling it.

Whenever someone in your life affects you negatively, you can be sure you have a toxic cord attached to them. You will feel drained, stressed out, or uncomfortable whenever they are around you. When the thought of them approaching you makes your stomach turn, then you can be sure you have a tough, nasty cord connected to them.

This cord attachment is placed between romantic partners or potential dates as well. Let's say someone is chasing a guy or girl who is not romantically interested in them. You start to check that person's social networking page daily for weeks. This is followed by a negative cord of attachment to that person. You grow to obsess over it to the point where it has taken over your life in an unhealthy way. Married couples, roommates, and anyone who lives together form cords of attachments. This is why some couples are so in tune to how the other is feeling. Both of the lights around your souls have connected and merged. Even if one of you is living in another city - the cord is still there. This is why you need to make sure that you and your partner are aiming to practice living a life of joy in your individual lives. If one of you is experiencing constant negativity, then the other partner will absorb that causing your cord between one another to become polluted. This is draining and can even cause you to have incessant arguments or to ultimately break up! One of the many points of a relationship is that you support and lift your partner up when they're experiencing discord.

It's important to cut cords regularly to certain relationships due to the buildup of dirty energy. This doesn't mean that you are cutting them out of your life necessarily, unless this is what you choose. You are removing the dysfunction or toxic part of the relationship.

What I have discovered while cutting cords is that my Guides and Angels will either remove and eliminate that person out of my life or improve the relationship. They eliminate them if they know there is no additional purpose or lessons needed to happen with that particular connection. Your Guides and Angels will remove the person in question if the lessons you need to gain with them are completed. They will also remove them if that person is still hanging around causing you turmoil. This can simultaneously hold you back from moving forward. Your vibration has risen while the other person remains buried under a lower vibration. They are not intending to deplete your energy, but this is what is happening regardless since you are made up of energy. If you are a sensitive person, then you are especially susceptible to the repercussions of forming an attachment to a negative and toxic person. I cut cords to certain people as part of my daily morning ritual. I mentally cut cords throughout the day if I need immediate cord cutting intervention with someone hostile or draining around me.

Sometimes when you work with certain people who are toxic it may be difficult to get rid of them. This is where some of the uninvited contamination in your aura happens. The second place is at home if you are living with others. This is why it important to do your best to ask that you be guided to work or live with high vibrational people. If you are unable to live alone, request to live with similar higher vibrational people who are peace loving souls. You will need to raise your vibration and keep that energy in your vicinity in order to attract in someone of a high caliber. High vibrational people can sense someone who is not of integrity or who is going to be a problem from a mile away.

If you are in a loving, committed relationship with someone and you are living together, then you have formed a cord. If the relationship is based on 100% pure love and compassion, then the cord will not be as dirty, but there will be a cord. You still need to keep some form of detachment so as not to fall into a position of co-dependency since the cord can get a little dusty. Those that you have formed a cord attachment with are not purposely attempting to drain your energy or spit toxins into you. They are unaware they are doing this. You are your own barometer gauge to know how certain people affect you. Do not forget that this is your soul to protect and it is up to you to manage it. You have the assistance of God, your angels, guides, and archangels within reach for this process. All you have to do is ask for their help. You don't need to chant some complex invocation. Saying something like this has invited in heavenly help: *"Okay, Archangel Michael I need your help with this..."*

As you begin cutting cords, then you will find methods that you're comfortable with that work for you. You can think the word *"angels"* and you are heard and have invited them in. One way I say it is:

"Please cut the cords between (so & so) and I."

List the people that you find to be toxic and draining. Say one person's name at a time. Take a deep breath in and exhale after each name. Do this by visualizing Archangel Michael taking his light sword and slicing the cord away between you and this other person. The people you list are those you know you will have to deal with or face that day and you definitely do not want to. Sometimes it might just be one person, while other times it's a few. There are some whom you will have to cut cords with every single day until they are gone from your life or the connection improves. When you find a connection is putting you in a repeated negative place, then cut the cords immediately. There are those you love and are close to, and you do not want them to go away, but you do not want any pain or dysfunction in your world anymore either.

For those cases you could say something like this:

"Please cut the cords between (the person) and I. Only remove the toxic, fear and dysfunction from this relationship, but keep the love and lessons."

When I've requested that the dysfunction be removed, I have found those relationships drastically improve or they elevate into something better. I hear Archangel Michael cutting the cords with one slash of his light sword. If it is a difficult cord that's hard as cement, he will continue cutting every day until it is removed. This can work with someone you're involved with romantically. If you find yourself not trusting them, and yet you have no valid proof to be reacting this way, then you will want to cut the cords with them. Some are afraid to do that because they fear that the person they love will be taken away. Having the cords cut does not necessarily mean they will be banished from your life. Your Guides and Angels will take care of the when and how. They will make the decision that benefits your higher self's path. All you need to do is ask for assistance. There is no reason to endure negative insecurities with anyone including a romantic partner.

I have had cases in the past where I was stuck having to deal with someone I did not want around me. This might have been an acquaintance or colleague that was toxic, negative or a gossip - all of which I will have no part of. It was pushed to the point where I was done with them. I had no interest and they offered nothing to me in the way of progress or growth, but merely contributed to heightened negative feelings. For those special cases I am quite firm in my cord cutting and even angry if nothing has been done about it. The angels are egoless and see your true light and nature. They do not take anything personally such as you stomping your feet in aggression. Not that I'm advocating that you do that, but there have been times where you are pushed to the edge and scream out for help.

"That's it! I want you to cut the cords between (the person's name) and I. Remove them from my life in all directions of time. Thank you."

I will immediately begin to see that our connection is elevated to a level that I can tolerate or they are removed from my life permanently.

Sometimes it's a process to extricate some people out of your life. The improvement might not be right away. I have witnessed changes and shifts happen over a period of time for some cases. Suddenly that person is let go from their job, they decide to leave and move on, or you have been moved away from them. The angels are maneuvering obstacles in the way. This is in order to bring about the changes you wish for that benefits your higher soul. They might be working behind the scenes with the other person's guardian angels to enact positive changes that benefit all parties involved. In the meantime, continue cutting those cords to that person every day until they are gone, or you are seeing an improvement in your connection with them.

Working lower energy jobs, while attempting to grow your light and become spiritually evolved can be challenging. You might have to deal with someone who can be disconnected from the real reality and living in full on arrogant ego mode. They are extremely deadly to you, your environment, and well-being. You could be working at the greatest place on Earth with wonderful colleagues, but there might be one or two bad apples who you might love to toss out a window. Every time you turn around they are standing there. They might be pushing your buttons in a negative way or getting under your skin. This is where cutting cords works beautifully. These are people you have to cut cords to every single day. They may not always be extricated from your life immediately, but you will start noticing them become a bit more tolerable and eventually off your radar. You form a cord of attachment to anything that is made up of energy. This means that cords can also be formed with material items such as your home, car or any other material items that you hold dear to your heart. You form cords to your feelings and emotions too. Cord cutting is a positive lifestyle trait you're adopting and incorporating regularly. Be aware of what you are attached to, as that is a clue where the cords exist.

SHIELDING

I am a sensitive who grew to have immense social anxiety due to a volatile upbringing. With the help of my Spirit team I was able to bring my social anxiety down to a manageable level. However, at the time of this book, I also function in an unpredictable and somewhat soulless city. You take unstable people and give them a machine to roam around in and control, such as a car, then you have a full-blown battlefield on the streets. The energy is worse than the anger of a murdering terrorist. This is why it is important to shield yourself. Shielding is another beneficial process to incorporate especially if you are a sensitive person. Sensitive people absorb energy emanating off of others like a muddy kitchen mop.

Take a deep breath in and exhale out. Call upon God and Archangel Michael. Ask him to shield you with bright white light for protection. Visualize a cocoon of white light surrounding you. This will keep out those nasty pests that insist on entering your field. The people you work for, or whom you are around regularly can be the greatest people, but even great people get moody, agitated and out of line. You sense this energy and vibration and it suddenly lowers yours. See the innocence and humor in other people, and do not let their drama and moods affect you.

Be wary of over shielding yourself, or business to the point where all are invisible. To avoid that from happening, ask to be surrounded by a *permeable* white shield of light allowing only the love to infiltrate.

You can request and envision different colored shields of light around you. These heavenly lights can be layered together or on its own. Your soul and aura is six feet tall, which is why your soul is literally too big for your body. It is important to be aware of it, sense it, and take care of what enters your auric field. The shields of heavenly light last up to 12 hours so you will need to do it daily as needed.

- ❖ *White* – Strongest light that protects you. Nothing can penetrate this shield.
- ❖ *Rose/Pink* – Offers protection while allowing only the love to enter your auric field.
- ❖ *Emerald Green* – Heals you in all ways such as physically, mentally or emotionally.
- ❖ *Violet* – Assists in raising your spiritual gifts and psychic sight.
- ❖ *Gold* – Powerful. Brings in God's love and light. Blasts away and repels all traces of negative thoughts and your lower self from your mind and body.

Remember to ask for help from your Guides and Angels. Even if you've been asking for help, you haven't seen results, and are losing faith – keep on asking and putting that energy out there. They are not ignoring you. If it is not happening right away there is a reason, but it will happen. There are obstacles and barriers being removed that are in the way to get you to that place you want to be in. Pay attention and listen for the signs that they might be giving you as well. They may be answering and advising you, but you are not paying any attention to it as you're expecting the answer to take a different form. If you are receiving a repetitive sign that happens more than three times and benefits your higher self, then you are receiving heavenly messages. They want you to be at peace. They want you to have enough time and resources to be able to focus and work on your life purpose. They do not want you to feel stuck at a dead end job struggling to make ends meet for all eternity. Start working with God and your Spirit team today to improve your life one-step at a time.

DISENGAGE FROM ANGUISH

Steer clear of everyone else's irrelevant drama. It doesn't do you or anybody any good to get involved with someone's ego. Someone else's stuff is not yours to absorb. You cannot learn other people's lessons for them. If a hostile person is continuously unloading their drama on you, stop responding, ignore them and walk away. You are the manager of your soul and life.

Human souls do not take enough breaks. The few holidays they are given the time off, they spend it tired or wasted in a toxic haze. When everyone is back to what they consider to be the grind or mundane, they are reminded of how unhappy they are with some part of their life. *(i.e. job, relationships, finances)* The edgy, angry feelings they had surrounding their current lives and in feeling stagnant rise once again. The slightest issue can be blown out of proportion and you might be caught in the line of that fire. Remove yourself from the racket if you find yourself being a target of someone else's blow up. Always revert back to focusing on you and your higher path. Become the calm in the eye of the hurricane. As for those acting out, they are discontent with where they are at. They are receiving nudges from their own Spirit team to make long awaited adjustments to their life, but are ignoring those messages. That is not anyone's problem to solve, but their own. You want to disengage and detangle yourself from other people's misery. This doesn't mean you are to be cold hearted. You can still be supportive and compassionate by not attaching yourself to their drama.

ETHERIC CREATURES
GNAWING ON MY LIGHT

The same way that spiders are sensitive to vibrations on their web, I am equally sensitive to the vibrations in and around me. If you are a sensitive or in tune to Spirit you likely know what this is like. I cannot be in crowded environments or stand obtrusive noises such as traffic sounds or garbage cans banging around. Naturally I assume no one is a fan, but my not liking it borders beyond what the average soul seems to tolerate without issue. I have to close my windows for a few minutes, or cover my ears when a siren is going by or a super loud plane is flying overhead. Being a clairaudient heightens every sound around me beyond the norm too. It's much like a dog or animal who perks up at a sound that no one else can hear. The only loud sounds I can tolerate are music. Music is the sound that connects you with the other side. Positive, uplifting music raises your vibration. The other side enjoys riding on the notes of the music. This is where the greatest message input is found.

When my spiritual sight re-opened up wider after I had rid myself of negative ways of living, I found that I had a steady link and connection to the Spirit world. This was also when I began hearing what sounded like chattering. I knew it was not Heaven as the sound was creepy and uncomfortable. It would cut in and out as if it were a bad static phone reception. It wasn't long before I clairvoyantly saw these dark insects in my peripheral vision. My Spirit team wanted me to know that due to my sudden increase in psychic activity that I was attracting in a number of skittering little etheric creatures that nibble on positive energy. The more you study and grow your psychic abilities, the brighter the light that you give off becomes - both in your aura and as your soul footprint. These etheric creatures feed off random positive energies. As your light grows they are attracted into your vicinity. These creatures make a little skittering noise like squirrels chattering. They were distracting me on a level that I wasn't fully aware of immediately and this caused a subtle change in my focus. These annoying little pests would break up my concentration. They would keep my subconscious mind from working on the walls and barriers I erected to protect myself from emotional damage. My Guides and Angels explained that I had full knowledge of suitable aura protection methods, but that I was not using them consistently enough. This allowed these little pests to get in.

I used to be lazy when it came to shielding and protecting my soul. That was until I had invited in an army of negative pests. Don't underestimate the value of soul protection, because if these little pests can penetrate your armor, some bigger bad bods can do more than just distract you. This is in no way meant to scare you. No one is in immediate danger from anything on this level. As you continue to study or grow your psychic abilities, and raise your vibration, you can become the target of larger entities that require bigger feeding stations, and this can get to be pretty draining.

A certain level of my consciousness was distracted by the ebb and flow of the spiritual work that I was doing more of. Combine this with the annoying little pests that were nibbling at my energy. I was not quite aware of who or what is and was coming into my immediate path during the pivotal spiritual transition. I could hear the little skittering noises of these psychic pests, which can be likened to that of a buzzing bee. When you hear them it will confirm their presence for you. If you choose to take action without the confirmation, then you need to bump up your protection visualizations morning and night. This can be as simple as envisioning an armor of golden light of protection around you and make that absolutely impermeable. Visualize yourself completely surrounded and utterly sealed off to anything except 100% positive energy. Believe that you are protected against all incoming energies that try to drain your psychic, mental and emotional energies. Affirm three times each session that you are protected and armored against these intrusions. See yourself as unbreakable!

The heavenly white light energizes whatever is in it. If it's an entity made up of negative and evil darkness, then the white light will literally cause an explosion when it meets its opposite. The entity will disappear and leave. I had experimented with this by pushing a few of those little mosquito-type chattering annoyances into it as you would push something in the water away from you. They would pop like popcorn to demonstrate their change in polarity.

If you are going to grow your light and expand your consciousness, awareness, place and work in this world, you will attract those who will try to stop you from doing this. It doesn't mean you're in danger. It just means you need to be aware of this and practice safe psychic study. Nothing is free as there is always an exchange of energy for energy. The more light you give off the more darkness you attract. The more you know and grow, the more attractive you and the light you give off becomes. It's like putting a low watt bulb on your porch and having a few moths attracted to it. It is that versus putting a 100-watt bulb out there and having every single insect of all varieties within a 10-block radius coming to gobble up the heat, light, and any other food they can find there. You're drawing in more of those energy eaters.

My higher self and soul grew to be so bright and intense with blasting white light that the darkness was extremely attracted to it. Think of it as mosquitoes buzzing around a tasty human wanting to take a drink of the yummy blood. They are dark bugs drawn to a blazing flame. I was dinner and those nasty dark beings wanted to get in and drain my delicious positive white light energy from me. This is why it's important for you to cleanse yourself with white light and seal your aura with gold light. Having the intention and visualizing this can do the job. You can find various instructions online on how to do this. Ask for guidance on the right way to do it. You'll know it's the right one when you experience positive vibes about what you've stumbled upon. Once you build that better suit of armor around your soul, then you will be able to concentrate on your own interior work, knowing that you are safe from all nefarious incomers.

Regardless of where I, or you, came from, you are here in your body now. The brighter your light shines, the more you draw in negative energy. If you are in the middle of a spiritual awakening or transition, then you are at the beginning of an important journey. Don't rush it because it takes years and lifetimes to master. You have been truly blessed with your own gifts and abilities whether you are aware of them or not. What you do with them in this lifetime is up to you. You have the opportunity to do great good in the world in the subtlest of ways. This is by allowing your light to shine in a way that is not harmful to you or anyone else. This light can infuse everything you do. By learning about it and yourself, you will allow more light to come into the world. The world is always in need of more light to keep the balance between the light and the darkness. If you never do anything else, but let your loving energy shine through to the world, that will be enough to help combat all the evil in the world.

Divine Timing

Heaven wants you to experience contentment and to not suffer, but they can only help you achieve this when you invite them into your life and begin working with them regularly. I began testing them out as I was growing up. I received incredible results in the process and was wowed becoming a true believer. Some may call it coincidence, but how can you call something coincidence that happens consistently every time you ask for something over a period of decades?

The more you work with them, then the more your life begins to change in positive ways. You find that your friendships and relationships begin to shift and improve. Those that were toxic and negative to begin with start exiting your life or you drift apart. It is not that you are repelling them, but they are repelling you! What once attracted you to them is no longer the case. You no longer feel a rush out of gossip, negativity, addictions or destruction anymore. This process can take what seems like a long while, but know that it is all happening and in motion. The angels are working with you on eliminating these people that no longer serve your higher purpose. Your vibration rises in the process. As that happens, you find that you are living the life you always wanted or you're heading towards it rather quickly.

There is always some measure of turmoil or tantrums whenever change happens with human souls. Trust the changes have a greater benefit to you in the end. Have patience and faith that it will. Everyone wants things now-now-now and I'm certainly no exception. You can make things easier on yourself when you know there are good reasons for things not happening right away and trust that it will come on its own time.

Sometimes there are lessons that you need to learn before you are shown the next move. Take a step back and pause. Move within for the answer. This is also known as your intuition. Notice what answers come to you on the situation you are questioning. Request that your Spirit team remove your ego as you tune into the messages being relayed to you. You will discover why there has been no change in your life yet. You may find that your lessons have been learned and there is nothing more to gain, but the delay in movement is because your Guides and Angels are working diligently behind the scenes to make it happen for you. There are circumstances that need to occur first on the other end before anything can happen.

An example might be, let's say that you are unhappy in the apartment you are living in and have asked for help in finding a new place of residence. You can't understand what the delay is in receiving that help. What you may not realize is that you have an idea of what apartment you're going to move into, but your Spirit team sees an even better scenario. They see you in an actual home of your own in an area you have only dreamt about, but brushed off as impossible. Yet, you deny this possibility because you do not believe you could ever own a home in this current market and with your financial status. They see something bigger entirely up ahead for you. They see a big sell with a project they have been assisting you with for some time. You do not see the potential financial gain, but they do which enables you to purchase that home. They may see you moving in with a potential love partner you've been dating or will be dating soon. This move takes place in an entirely different part of town. If you jump towards something out of impatience you could potentially throw your path off course and cause an even greater delay.

Your ego is fixated on nabbing something immediately and talks you into jumping. It sounds like a great idea to you at first. You later wished you had exercised more patience for the real excellent stuff. Delays are for good reason so that other pieces of the puzzle can be put into place and maneuvered into something far greater than you imagined.

When you meditate, take pause, or move into a daydream as you connect to your Spirit team. You can discover what they are currently working on for you in this state. Your Guides and Angels always see you as being more capable than you see yourself. If you are receiving messages that seem far-fetched, then it is important that you remember to have faith and trust in it. You have abilities that you might be discrediting as impractical. Heaven knows what you are capable of. Your soul was born into this life with the capability of wonderful magnificence.

THE WHITE LIGHT

White light is the color of spirit, purity, transformation and completion. All human souls have been changing whether they recognize this or not. They have been bringing their previous lives to a close by shedding anything and everything that has blocked or prevented them from welcoming in new and brighter circumstances. Some do not have a choice. The universe is forcing it on all of humanity. There are some who may stomp their feet, or sulk, since change can feel uncomfortable. Your Spirit team is assisting you more than ever to make this change. They are also bringing souls to you in human form to enlighten and change you. The answers you need are coming from the source and the white light within you. Tune into it, embrace it, and follow it. It has always been there and it has always been this way since you came to being. This white light has been kicked up a notch and is targeted globally. Many souls are looking and longing for answers. Some of them are seeking out some form of spirituality since it is more compassionate and open hearted. You cannot wander around oblivious in your life anymore and nor can you can ignore it. This white light is growing around the globe. More people of this white light are being born to usher it along so that it will be spread like wildfire. We are banishing the darkness in humanity. It is no longer acceptable behavior to be cruel or to be operating from pure ego.

Chapter Five

LAW OF ATTRACTION

Successful people have at least one thing in common. They are optimistic when it comes to what they want to achieve. They fixate on their desire with unwavering strength and focus. Heaven does not want you to suffer, but your ego will do whatever it takes to ensure you experience downfall. Heaven and your team of Guides and Angels understand that you have basic human needs. When you are happy and fulfilled in all areas of your life, your Spirit team knows that you are more apt to focusing on your life's purpose. The daily choices you make can block the flow of abundance without you realizing it. Sometimes it can be a perpetual cycle of negative thoughts that run through your mind. Perhaps you sit in traffic every day to and from work with anger or stress. This negative mindset constructs a block on your road to abundance. Your words and thoughts have a powerful energy vibration. It effortlessly brings you something of equal value. If your words and thoughts are mostly negative, then this is what you're going to bring to you. You either bring in more negative circumstances to you, or you bring in nothing. These are the human souls that complain that it feels as if they've been stagnant forever with little to no movement. If you spend your entire day doing nothing or partaking in time wasting activities of a low vibration, then you have made a choice. All of your choices have a cause and effect in what is to come to you. Take note when you made a decision in your past that potentially altered your intended course. You may be able to recall how this choice caused a preferred or undesired effect. The goal is to be aware of your thoughts, words and the choices you make throughout your day. This is how to stop yourself from making a decision that you know will set off an entire array of unwanted results. When you connect and tune in with your own higher self, then you become fully conscious of the choices you make. If you make a decision that you know deep down is going to cause unhappiness to yourself or someone else, then re-consider your approach. Notice how unnecessary the choice might be when compared to the ultimate outcome. Your lower self and ego makes choices in haste, or in an impulsive burst of suffocating energy. It is bathed in overwhelming negative emotion and then this is what you bring more of to you.

Allow any damaging baggage in your life to

fade away. Carefully plan the next few years of your life. When deep in thought or meditation, focus in on what it is you dream of or desire. For example, say a positive affirmation such as, "I'm going to buy a home that will be the foundation of my life." Ask your Spirit team for help with this. Tell them what you want and give them an area, "I will buy an affordable Condo in this area and here's how much money I have." Sit down with your Spirit team and visualize what you want with them. Envision exactly how you want your life to be in a year. Before you know it, it will be the end of the year and it will be exactly that. Human souls need steady, stability and calm. This state of mind is the perfect breeding ground to raise your vibration and attract in positive abundance. Love yourself and all the good that you have within you, because you are awesome!

VISUALIZING YOUR REALITY

Visualize how you want your life to be. Even if it seems impossible, do it anyway. Feel it in your gut and in every cell of your body. Believe it as if it is already happening. This can be from the career you want, relationship, home, or anything you desire pending it is not harmful to you or someone else. Aligning it with your higher self's purpose is the way to create good Karma. Visualizing circumstances that are harmful to you or someone else is dangerous. It will backfire and become part of your Karmic thread, even if it is initially a success. Eventually it is a debt that has incurred on your soul that must be paid back. When someone's ego wants something with great veracity, then it is not in a high vibrational state of mind to understand the consequences until it's too late. Never discredit the power of your mind. You have the power to create your reality. You are creating your reality whether you're fully aware of this or not. You can have anything you want as long as you hold the intention with positive thoughts. Allow your mind to wander into a daydream visualizing the life you want. Remember that if a thought has any doubt in it, then this can negate or delay what you want from happening. Therefore it is important to catch yourself when distrust creeps into your mind. When this happens and you are aware of it, then mentally say, "Cancel that thought and replace it with this." Modify the negative thought with something positive in exchange.

Some of history's immense talents, leaders and CEO's are in the positions they're in because they do not allow insecurity or negative self-talk to stop them from accomplishing what they intend to. They set intentions without negative interference. They know exactly what they want with unwavering excitement surrounding this desire. They go after it with enormous gusto and they get it! If you witness successful leaders in action, you will find they are precise, focused and optimistic.

THOUGHTS PRODUCE CIRCUMSTANCES

Negative thoughts cause the majority of human unhappiness. It is true that challenges happen for a reason. If you do not have challenges, then you do not learn, grow and overcome. When you are aware of the challenges, then you are able to shift them into something positive. Being aware of them is to have an understanding of why a challenge took place. Avoid losing sight of what is important on your journey here. It is easy to veer off track when functioning in this material based world on a regular basis. Take a little bit of time out daily to detach from the chaos around you. This is to avoid permanently drowning in the ego based noise of the world. Days pass by and you discover you are going through the motions. Your thoughts move into words of a lower vibration, thus bringing more of this to you.

You are always creating your own future reality. When bathed in negative thoughts, it will soon make it seem as if nothing is going your way. Suddenly you receive a parking ticket, or you get into a car accident, or you are pulled over. Next thing you know you are running into one person after another who is making you feel even more miserable. It turns into a domino effect that continues forward without any hope of escape. You become immersed in it to the point where you're oblivious to the fact that you created this reality. This consistent negative reality persists for weeks. You complain about it with anyone who will listen from friends, family, to colleagues. This lowers their vibration in the process. Those around you soak up this energy since it latches onto their aura. They begin to exude this same behavior and spread it around to others as well. You can see how this can get out of hand. A movement of this negative outbreak infects the entire planet. For some, this carries on for years and even decades! They do not believe they are the cause of this and therefore are unaware that they have the power to stop this cycle. This is why no one can deny the planet is in complete chaotic angry disarray. Turn on the media or visit a social networking site. Most of it contains a diatribe of complaints.

The words are easy to detect because they can be negative, judgmental, critical and abusive towards yourself or others. The reason that we use the word vibration or energy is because they are invisible particles in the air that many might not be accustomed to understand. Human ego believes something to be non-existent if it is unseen. You have more power than you realize. You have the power to manipulate this energy in your surroundings and bring forth to you that which you desire. Keep your thoughts and words high vibrational in order to attract in abundance.

If you find you're buried in negativity, then it is time for a soul time out. Escape from the noise around you and retreat to somewhere quiet. Close your eyes for a moment and relax. Take a deep breath in and exhale. Change the negative sentences, complaints, or worries which your mind is repeatedly stating. Shift them into something positive. You can do this by starting your sentences with, "I love…"

"I love myself. I love who I am. I love that I have a car that runs. I love that I have a job that pays all my bills." And so forth.

Practice shifting your words to those of gratitude. If you find you're moving back into negativity and destructive thoughts, then be conscious of this and shift it once again. Re-word your sentences to more positive uplifting ones. It is work re-training your mind to get to that place, but with practice and over time, you will get better at it. The results will be astounding when you find that great things begin coming your way. You discover that your life has become less stressful. Negativity is a learned trait. Most of it stems from childhood conditioning. You unknowingly adopt it as second nature. This is why breaking those bad habits down or diminishing them can take some time and work on your part to bring your soul to the high vibrational space it was when you were first born.

The Archangel Michael vacuums away all dark energy. Visualize him holding an ethereal vacuum hose. He takes this hose and inserts it into your crown chakra above your head and down into your body. Imagine that he turns the vacuum on and sucks out any negative, dirty ion debris lodged within and around your body. Some of this negativity hardens if you've been harboring it for some time. Allow him to remove all traces of this toxic negativity within and around your body and soul leaving you feeling uplifted and optimistic. Let go of all burdens and concerns and hand it over to him for transmutation. Once you release the need to control the outcome of your worries, the more likely it will resolve itself in a rapid fashion. If you have been hanging onto tons of negativity, then do this clearing daily until you know or sense that it is gone. At that point, you will be much better at managing it and extricating it from your vicinity when it happens again. It is advised to do a routine cleaning once in awhile if you live in a heavily populated area, since this is where negative energy expands on a daily basis.

DAYDREAM

Avoid getting caught up in the noise and drama of the world's nasty behavior. Human drama flies out from all angles on a regular basis. It is erratic and unstable. It does nothing to help you or anybody. Take regular time outs than necessary, and relax and smile more. Shun going to places where you know it is going to be taxing on your system. Go for walks alone *(or with a love interest)* and daydream. Do this in a nature setting if possible. Daydream about beautiful, wonderful circumstances and feelings. Think about the amazing blessings you currently have, and then daydream about what you would like to see manifest next in your life. If your life is where you want it, then daydream about that more. Take walks in areas where you know it will not be crowded with people. I've witnessed others attempting to go for a stroll in busy cities only to dodge restless and reckless drivers nearly running them over. You're on guard and your heart rate shoots up on high alert every time you have to cross a busy street with impatient drivers. This is no way to relax and center your soul. Venture off into a nature setting whenever possible for strong effectiveness. Find a quiet place to focus or meditate on anything that is not man-made. This can be something like a sunset, a plant, flower, or mountain peak.

The moon phases and cycles have a larger energy power behind them. Check online or a planetary calendar for the dates of the New Moon and Full Moon phases. Most calendars tend to have those two transits listed for each month. The New and Full Moon transits add extra manifesting energy to your thoughts. Be careful with your thoughts more than usual during those moon phases. Keep them positive and upbeat. If your mind goes into worry or something negative, you are going to bring about more of that to you! The New Moon is a great time to start a new positive activity or regimen. This can be beginning a new relationship, job or even sending out your resume. The New Moon symbolizes new beginnings. The Full Moon has immense manifestation power as well. The Full Moon is typically a nice phase to release bad habits or people, while aligning your focus with what you truly desire.

Do whatever it takes to get you to that place of feeling happy and content. This can be anything small from watching a funny, uplifting movie, to hanging out with a cheerful friend who always makes you laugh. Place your work and worries aside and celebrate your life. Be grateful for what you currently have. See your soul and where you're at in a positive light. See the blessings that you have in your life right now. Do not think about or worry over what is coming next or what is not here. Put that all aside and let loose and enjoy yourself. Learn to celebrate this life and insist on having more good times.

It is inevitable that you will hit a rough patch in your Earthly life. This might be where your soul feels lost, overly emotional, or lethargic. Sometimes these feelings signify that you are on the precipice of grand changes needing to happen in your life. It is a transformative period prompting you to be more introspective. What matters is how you work through the issues that this energy is bringing out of you. What it creates within you might be uncomfortable as it is asking you to examine where you are at in your life. This can be in any area such as career, relationships or health.

Learn from your current circumstances, choices and experiences. Avoid remaining mired in negative feelings and thoughts. Heavy emotions force you to be hyper-focused on where you are at. This prompts you to feel stuck as if you are trapped in an eternal prison. Yucky feelings stall your progress and forward movement. It becomes difficult to reach a place of happiness while in that state. In order to work through these feelings and thoughts, you have to examine them with a fine toothcomb. Look for the underlying cause and message that continues to prompt you to obsess over thoughts which have no basis in reality. What areas in your life are provoking you in a negative way? Those are areas which require a necessary change. Ask your Spirit team for assistance and follow their guidance, even if they push you out of your element. Know they do this for your own higher self's good. It is a sign that it is a time to move on to the next plateau. See only the love and lessons in the experiences you are asked to modify or leave. Make your peace with it in order to move to a brighter, content life.

MONEY, SUCCESS, ABUNDANCE

Everyone deserves to live comfortably without worry. Even if you're twenty years old, create supplemental and retirement income today. Before you know it, you will be forty years old and wonder why you had not started earlier. When you take one action step at a time towards your goal, you will be that much closer to seeing your dream happen. One of the positives of the modern day world we live in is that everything is at your disposal. It is not like earlier history, or the 20th Century, where everyone had to rely on corporate greed to have the opportunities to express their talents. Those days are no more and thank God. You are able to go out there and put it together yourself at any age. The plusses of the digital world are that it allows one to successfully work for themselves.

All human souls want to live comfortably happy. This is in knowing that your bills are paid on time without any struggle while having more time to pursue personal luxuries and focus on your purpose here. Sometimes it might feel like you are taking a step forward and then a step back. This is much like the image of a spiral staircase. You are not going backwards or having a setback. Rather you are going around and then up.

When you focus your sole attention on obtaining money, then you shut off the supply. Do not believe that money is your security. Look to God as your source of security. This is how abundant manifestation flows freely. You work for, "God, Incorporated." When you need supplies, then you ask for it. It is only when you say the words with intent that it soon takes form. Success is not always financial. It can be a state of mind where you feel grateful and are optimistic with what you have, where you are at and how far you have come. It is to take note of the great progress you have made to date.

Understand that money is only paper. Back around the B.C. ages, humankind created money by using things like sticks and stones. This was in order to obtain certain living essentials. We were not paying for these necessities, but rather exchanging it for goods. There is an exchange of energy. You're giving something to receive something. Soon the sticks and stones were manufactured into paper with dollar amounts and symbols on it. Human ego placed great emphasis and need on this paper. This pushed it further away from them. The real moneymaker is your higher self, the YOU of all you, God, the source, whatever you want to call it. Your thinking and limited reasoning mind is not. Let that all go and focus on the source for your abundance. Say affirmations such as: *"All of my needs and supplies are met in every way and in all directions of time."*

MANIFESTING

The key to manifesting is having an unwavering passion for a desire. You can have anything you want and can cause anything to happen when you have unbending passion for it. This is where you feel this passion for your desire all over you, within you, and around you. You feel and know it in your mind. You feel and know it in your heart. You feel and know it all throughout your body and soul. You know without a doubt that it will happen and that it is here now. It's allowing this feeling to build to the intensity of an erupting volcano. You feel this desire continue to rise with positive excitement from within. There are no negative feelings associated with this passionate feeling. You visually see what you want happening in reality with great optimism. If you are having a passion for obtaining something, but you have doubts circling that, then the doubts will overpower the desire and you will receive the doubts instead of the desire. Experience inner peace and uplifting joy that you're living this vision as if it is real time. It is seeing this vision as if it is here and happening now. Hold this intention everyday and avoid negative thoughts from taking over. It is not enough to visualize something you want, but to also take action steps to get there. When you have a passion for something, you naturally want to dive into that passion. Having passion is a joyous feeling. It's the key to manifesting positively.

Once this is complete, the most difficult step is to then let it go. It's to release this vision and desire of what you want to your higher self, God, or your Spirit team. It's completely letting go of this desire and not caring about it. It's releasing and surrendering it to a higher power. The reason this is a challenging step is because most people find it difficult to let go of something they really want. They fixate on it heavily never letting the desire go. This then moves into obsessive doubts and concerns that it will never happen. However, if this last step is not followed, and you do not let this desire go and release it, then the manifestation connection is not fully made. It may push the outcome further away from you. This gives you an idea as to why your desire is not coming to fruition. You must let it go and move onto the next manifestation. Do not concern yourself with the how or when a manifestation will occur as this will block it. If you obsess over a desire, then you will block it from manifesting. Instead, you will receive negative manifestations or you'll find that you're in a stagnant position where there is no movement at all.

I've always been manifesting, as everyone is manifesting whether they're aware of it or not. I've been manifesting since I was a teenager through this process I describe. When I was sixteen, I knew I would be an author, but I also knew I would have to obtain a regular job first. I needed a steady income. If I were attempting to work on my dream as an author while worrying about not having a paycheck, then this would block me from achieving this dream. My Spirit team revealed the film business to me. They let me know that I would get a job in the creative side of the business, where I'd incorporate my love for storytelling and writing. I knew I was going to get into the entertainment business and nothing was going to stop me. When I was sixteen years old my mantra was: "I'll keep trying to get in until I'm 80." I studied books about the business and then went after notable production companies at full force. I got in the door right after my 23rd birthday. This was when I started working for one of the top ten most bankable and popular actresses at that time. Not surprisingly one of my main roles for her was to read scripts and provide written coverage or a synopsis on the work. I graduated from that particular class, after she dissolved her production company. I then made a move into coordinating film production shoots for the major studios. This was followed by me making the transition into work as an author. This is the quick cliff note version, but hammers home that I knew what I wanted with a burning desire, I went after it and got it.

Many struggling to get into Hollywood have always asked me what my secret was to getting in. I was passionate about it. I knew I was going to get into the industry. I had a steady, calm, euphoric positive energy surrounding what I wanted. I use the word passion to describe this process. If you don't have passion for something, then it will show. It doesn't matter what your expertise is or what kind of degree you have. None of that matters. If you have no passion and it shows, then you can forget about attracting your desire in. You need to passionately want it, but then let go of knowing, how or when it will happen.

When I first started out in the entertainment business, I had no skills or experience to warrant getting a job in that industry. All I had to sell them was my personality, drive and passion. I walked in there and conveyed how much I wanted it and how right I was for the gig. There was no acting needed, because I genuinely wanted it with incredible veracity. I went after every job position with this same passion and I was hired. This same manifestation process was the same process for how I became an author. I knew I was going to do it. I clairvoyantly saw it up ahead. I've been following my own Spirit team's guidance, messages, and steps relayed to me from as far back as a teenager. This same process was also the case with all of the relationships I was involved in. I knew without a doubt that I would be with a particular person. Granted, I'm sure in hindsight, I might have paid bigger attention to the red flags presented, but the point is to be careful what you wish for. If the wish is felt with great positive veracity, passion, and steadfast intensity, then you will get it!

LIFE PURPOSE

Your life purpose is an interesting dichotomy in figuring out what it is. It can be what you love doing more than anything in the world. It can also be whatever makes you angry or riles you up. For example, someone who is always getting upset or angry when people throw trash in the ocean. They were meant to come here to do something about it such as joining in with an environmental organization, start a blog, or mobilize to clean up the oceans. This is their life purpose.

To turn your hobby into a career, take action steps towards it daily. You can do this in baby steps. Spend at least thirty minutes a day diving into whatever it is you want to accomplish. If you are working on a book, then spend at least thirty minutes each day writing a page. The universe will meet you tenfold in manifesting your dreams. When you are working on what you love, then it doesn't feel like a drag. You may be working at a job you're not happy with, but when you have something to look forward to at the end of the day, then it raises your vibration. This opens up the door for the universe to step in and meet you half way. You'll be that much closer to having your dream come true. It may feel like a struggle at first, but you will eventually notice the positive changes that are revealing itself to you in trickles over time. If you keep at it, then eventually that love will be your career! It will bring in enough financially that you're able to quit the job you're unhappy with. Ones hobby or love is often connected to their life purpose. However, a new human soul experiencing their first Earthly life may have a purpose that requires they learn patience or forgiveness. It might not be a specific "work" oriented goal, but it could be. It is up to them to discover this on their own.

When you are not at your job, what do you enjoy doing on your off time? What is your hobby? Is it painting? Is it singing or playing the guitar? Your hobby is not surfing the internet, heading to the bar with friends every other night, or shopping for clothes. Those are called distractions, time wasters and addiction feeders. Your hobby is an activity that you enjoy doing on your own. It's one that gives you an added skill or knowledge around a certain area that gives you pleasure. Your hobby is what you want to turn into a career.

Let's look at a couple of well-known entertainers in music history. Bruce Springsteen has been playing his guitar since he was a teenager. When he was playing the guitar in those days it was his hobby and something he enjoyed doing. He was able to transition that hobby into a full time career that lasted a lifetime. When Madonna was a teenager she enjoyed dancing. This was her hobby. She took classes and looked for work that would enable her to incorporate her love for dancing. She was able to broaden that into an even bigger career that has also lasted a lifetime. Music entertainers bring joy to the world and Heaven applauds this.

Many who work jobs that are not surrounding their hobby or passion, are more likely to be unhappy than those who are. I have been shown that those who are unhappy with their jobs tend to reach for addictions like alcohol, food or other toxic vices more than those who are happy with their work. Some of them reach for addictions like a caffeine fix mid-day. They will pop pills to tranquilize themselves to sleep at night and then ingest high doses of caffeine for an energy jolt to get them started every morning. You take something at night to calm down and sleep, and then you ingest something to infuse you with energy to get you going. The days where they are not at their job, like the weekend or a vacation day, they are less likely to reach for these substances. This is a clue that you are unhappy at your job, but are convincing yourself that this is just the way it is.

What don't you have that you wish you had? Is it a great career, love, or great health? Are you at a job you enjoy, but wish you were working at your dream career? Take time each day to work on your career while you work your day job. You will be that much closer to obtaining your dream. You will also have something to look forward to at the end of the day when you leave your job. When you spend at least thirty minutes a day diving into your hobby, then you are devoting time towards your passion.

If you keep making excuses that you're too tired or that you never have enough time, then you push your dream that much further away from you. The right time may never come unless you take control of your life by working this hobby into your schedule. I've worked two full time jobs that include my regular job and my career. It can be done if everything in your entire being loves this hobby. You can turn this into a career if it is work that you are interested in doing. Another clue is that this is work that you would do for free if you had all day to do it. Your finances are taken care of and you are completely settled and secure in every way. You are then able to spend time on this hobby because it gives you joy. The money that comes in from this work is just the icing on the cake.

How would you like to get paid for doing work that you love and have fun doing? It does not feel like work if it is something you love. This is also a sign that it is your life purpose. You should never quit your regular job until your hobby has turned into something lucrative enough that you know you will be able to survive financially.

Chapter Six

TRANSFORM YOUR WORK LIFE

*O*ne of the biggest complaints and grumblings I hear others protest about is how tired they always are. Feeling tired even when you are getting an average of eight hours of sleep a night can partially be a symptom of depression. You might not even realize you are depressed because you equate the 'depression' word to be associated with feeling down or someone prone to crying in despair. This is not true. Many work at jobs they hate or are unhappy at, while others are unemployed for a great deal of time. Some work at jobs that pay just enough to survive. Weeks, months and then years of this pass and the weight of these effects start to take its toll on you. Terribly unhappy with poor diets and lifestyle choices coax you onto reaching for bad foods and addictions in hopes of instantaneous comfort. The opposite is ego driven exercising, which is a form of addiction. This is when one merely works out to look desirable to others. When one is unhappy with their work life, it pushes them to reach for an addiction to keep going. Being unhappy in a relationship is significantly different. Those who are unhappy in a relationship will dive more into work or they leave their mate. When someone is unhappy at work, but their relationship is fine, they rarely dive into their relationship. For one, most people unhappy at work are working 40 hours a week, which is more time spent than anywhere else. The irony is that those who are unhappy find it easier to walk away from their love relationships in an impulse, but will stay at an unhappy job for years simply because it's paying the bills. You allow your job to rule you. Your job is paying your bills, but in the end when your soul crosses over, it becomes obsolete. What matters are the relationships you had with others that have more of a profound impact on your soul in the end. Your relationships are worth saving over an unhappy job.

More people resort to some form of anti-depressant or anti-anxiety medication than ever before. While there is nothing wrong with any form of medical treatment, you do want to make sure you are not on medication for the sole reason of shutting life out permanently. On the flip side, those who might be against anti-depression medication may be the ones who are abusing an unhealthy addiction to *numb the pain*. This would come in the guises of food, drugs, cigarettes or alcohol. No one around me knows more about numbing the pain than I do. I used to consume anything and everything that was bad for me in order to feel bliss if even temporarily. Often it was on purpose just to cause my soul harm. As much as there are benefits to taking anti-depressants for those who absolutely need them, the down side is that is what contributes to a zombie like emotionless state of mind. I am not advocating that you stay away from anti-depressants, because they do help a great deal of people who absolutely need them. Life has been tough for so many that they may be unable to pull through. Anti-depressants under the care of a physician can help restore and re-train your mind. The challenge is when you wane off the medication and attempt to forge on in life anti-depressant free. I was on anxiety medication for several years at one point in my life. They did help me get through two relationship break-ups with those who were emotionally unavailable. Those connections coaxed me to take back control of my life and not rely on someone else for my emotional comfort. It also prompted me to discover what I do not want in a love relationship. I would not accept anything less than stability, compassion, love, and trust in a romantic potential.

The average person works full time. This means they are working 40 hours a week, which is roughly 160 hours or so a month. A large chunk of your time is spent at a job every day with no end in sight. Ensure that you are participating in meaningful work that makes you happy. Couple that with you working with people that you have a positive synastry with. If one or either of those things is not in place, then you will fall into a stress-filled depression. Those unhappy at their job are afraid to leave. They fear dusting off their resume's, getting back out there and taking a chance in a new work place. They have bills to pay and they find some comfort in the security that the job they are at provides.

Perhaps your job is paying the bills and you appreciate that, yet you are still terribly unhappy inside. You are unfulfilled in your life. You're working at a job that you do not enjoy. You find you have to convince yourself to love it just to get through the day. There are several factors, which cause you to feel despondent. One of them can be that you hate the work you do. Perhaps you are stuck in a cubicle and would prefer to be working somewhere in the outdoors in nature. What is a redeeming feature is that you enjoy the people you work with and love the company. You have just enough to keep going, but is it enough?

What if you not only despise the work you are doing, but you also experience discomfort about one or more of the people you work with. You can be working with one person who you find antagonistic or pessimistic. They are toxic and negative in numerous ways. They can be abusive, which is the worst kind of person to be around. Not all abusive people are aware that they are this way. They are unhappy about where their life is too. This spills over to the rest of the staff. Then there is the narcissistic abusive colleague or boss. They are the ones that are aware they're abusive and yet they do not care. They believe that instilling fear is how to be powerful and exert their dominance. Exerting ones dominance through aggressive behavior comes from fear, which has zero power. This is the same trait that a bully has. It overcompensates in an attempt to cover up the real weakness they hide. Assertive and compassionate people have the highest vibrational power. They come off diplomatic and strong while winning respect and a team player attitude from others in the process.

You despise going into work and do not look forward to it, and yet you do it anyway. You do it because you are responsible and you have personal responsibilities to take care of, but inside you wonder if the horrid cycle will ever end. This downtrodden aura around you shows when you are at work, and then you bring it home to infect others you live with. You're the one the others in the office consider to be the unhappy camper. People who feel joy and contentment will shine and radiate. They are self-assured and lovable while still running an ordered ship. Find work that you love and avoid selling yourself out for a paycheck. Spending years at a job you despise will crush your spirit. This is heartbreaking and will keep your soul feeling trapped. Perhaps you work 160 hours a month at a job you despise, and on top of that you work with someone toxic. It is one thing if it is a colleague, but if it is your boss, then that adds an additional amount of issues weighing your soul down. Working at an unhappy job lowers your vibration and keeps it there until you break away from it. Breaking away from it can be through force, such as the company lays you off or fires you. You finally leave the company, or your soul gives out and you leave the Earth plane to head back home to Heaven.

Every morning the world sits in traffic attempting to race to work. You cannot race to work when you have endless cars in front of you moving at various speeds. For the most part, they are all riding with each other, but then you have the one person who is driving too slow or too fast. Everyone is a heart attack waiting to happen for many reasons. It is not just the obscene traffic. It must be stated since this is a common complaint among the 9-6 working class. They are either too tired from not enough sleep or they are fueled up on an abundant amount of caffeine and sugar. All of these exasperates and confuses your state of mind. When you are too tired, then you function in a haze. Your judgment is off and so are your thoughts and emotions. Pumping yourself up on high amounts of caffeine and sugar raises your blood pressure and causes hypertension, not to mention high levels of anxiety. You react erratically to every tiny little thing. This causes more unhappiness and blocks the communication lines from Heaven. The communication lines to Heaven are where the answers are to pull you out of this human designed trap.

The majority of people work in jobs they hate, or work with antagonistic and toxic people. You deal with at least one personality that never jives with your own. This is what your life has become.

This is what dominates your world since your job is where you're physically at most of the week. It is difficult to shake it off. You know you fall into this bracket when you leave work at the end of the day and you're too tired to do anything. Instead you head straight home to collapse while shielding yourself off from the noise of the world. If you are not going home, you are heading to the bar with colleagues or friends to decompress, vent or complain while drinking alcohol. Even the media perpetuates this ritual in entertainment where friends head to drink together at the bar to find bliss. This temporarily masks the issues and unhappiness. It does not permanently remove it. The next day the hole that has become your life is in plain view in front of you. If you are not meeting up with friends or colleagues for drinks after work, you are drinking at home to take the edge off. If you are in a relationship, you might take it out on your mate. However, if you are in a healthy love relationship, you may talk it over calmly. Couples in healthy relationships know about balancing the good with the bad. You retreat to each other feeling safe from the noise. Long term healthy love relationships raise your vibration just by being in each other's company and presence. Unfortunately, in this modern day progressive world, many complain they also find it difficult to find a long term loving relationship to begin with. Loyalty and commitment are lacking more than ever in history. This is what happens when your ego rules the roost. It wants to do what it wants you to do without any consequence or regard for others.

The ones that have it down are those who live in areas where there is a low population of people, living in or close to nature, and/or who work for themselves, and/or are in healthy long term love relationships. If you've got all of these, then you're likely in that space of beautiful contentment. There are those that love their job in the big city, but you do not love your job if whenever it is a workday you stress over the slightest disruption. It shows when you love your job. You are the one who is the calm within the storm. You are peaceful, centered and happy. All of these traits radiate around this person on a regular basis.

Tyler found that working a 9-6 job for someone else doing menial tasks only bored him. It was depressing and crushed his spirit little by little until he was permanently dejected. He would pump himself up with caffeine all day long. He did not drink soda or coffee, but he would use sports powders and B vitamin-energy powders so that he was at least getting some amino acids and vitamins. Although this is slightly better than soda, there are still other chemicals in there that should not be. They contributed to boosting his energy levels in some unnatural way. He would do this to pump himself up with excitement in order to gather enough energy to pretend to be into his job and get through the day. By the time the day was over, he would crash and collapse at home before he tranquilized himself to sleep at night. He would repeat this mantra the next day and so forth. Can you imagine the brevity of this behavior over the long-term?

The self-made prison he created was for a paycheck. He was grateful that he had a paycheck, but this Monday thru Friday ten hours a day drained him. He would wake up at around 7:00 every morning, fight traffic for a half an hour when it should be fifteen minutes. By the time he was back home and settled in, it was 7:00 at night. Sometimes it was eight at night or beyond if he made a stop at the gym or the store. He did not always feel like jumping in the shower to head out with friends. There was zero motivation for much else. He would have an hour or so left to eat and relax before he needed to wind down to get to bed at a decent hour. This is a minimum 8-hour sleep cycle requirement that everyone should aim for. Imagine how tired Tyler would be if he also had chosen to start a family with children. He would likely have to nix the strict 8 hour sleep schedule.

If you find that you are sleeping at least eight hours a night, and yet you are still tired, then you might have adrenal fatigue. This is that no matter how much sleep you get, you are still tired throughout the day. To get through each day, you stuff yourself with caffeine in any source you can get. This only masks an even bigger problem that includes you not being as happy as you think you are in your life. When you are happy, then you experience a natural uplifting high. It is an alert energy you access from God or Higher Power. You crave very little caffeine if any. The stresses of each day are hard on your system and this causes this type of fatigue. The depression symptoms are still there, because unhappy people have some measure of depression. Check with your doctor to make sure there are no potential issues within you beyond feeling tired and depressed around the clock. If you check out fine, then depression and adrenal fatigue may be the common ailment causing this low energy within you. Either way your doctor can adequately diagnose you. It is equally important to examine the trouble areas in your life that could be the underlying cause. When you ask for heavenly assistance, your Spirit team can guide you to the remedies that are beneficial for your case.

Americans specifically and some other parts of the world have this work and no play attitude. They have created a five-day work week when it should really be a four-day work week. Most people who work this type of schedule are not productive on Friday's. Some companies release their employee's mid-day on Friday. Many European countries do not observe the work them into the ground mentality. They have the four-day work week utilized. It is second nature to human souls to work five-day work weeks like dogs. This was programmed by the human ego.

Do you want to go out Friday night? Forget it. Many professionals have little to no energy for that unless it is work related and they have to. By the time the weekend rolls around, most of the working force spends Saturday running around playing catch up on practical matters. Sunday you cannot do much either since it is truly your only real day off. If you have families, then you know the demands of that time as well. Children see their parent or parents moping around the house exhausted and moody. When the uneventful weekend ends quickly, you dive right back into the unhappy work week angry and bitter. Years of this scenario pass by. You reminisce about what you wish your life could be like, and yet you never take any steps to get there.

Tyler wanted to have a career where he runs the show. He wanted successful self-employment, but he allowed negative thoughts to pervade him by asking questions like, "How many people actually get to do that?" As long as you have passion for it, then you can most certainly have that. Keep the faith and build your side business while working at your job. Remain optimistic and positive that the abundance will come in over time. When that happens, then you will be able to quit your day job and focus on your passion full time. You will be able to buy that house you have always wanted with an all cash offer. Home paid for and done!

Your future is changeable and psychically forecasted as probable. Due to your daily choices and actions, you might unknowingly alter your course with a decision or non-decision. You are the manager of your life. You are responsible for the choices you make. This is not saying that just because you find yourself in one toxic scenario after another that you are asking for it. It is a wake-up call to stop the cycle. The way to do that is to make different choices in your life. Break the pattern and make decisions that you might not normally make, or ones that might not be popular. Watch your life start to shift in a new, brighter way. Have faith that change is not only on the horizon, but that it is happening now. Accept that you will no longer be a victim of your circumstances.

If you are at an unhappy job, then start taking steps to change that. Schedule at least one day a week to explore your options for a new job. If you want to turn your hobby into a career, then start putting in some effort into it at least thirty minutes to an hour each day. Taking these steps and having a disciplined routine will start to raise your vibration and help you in attracting in the right kind of work for your temperament.

Ask your Spirit team on the other side for help. Tell them what you want and give them permission to intervene. You can say something like: *"Please help me find a great job that is aligned with my purpose. This is one that ensures all of my bills are paid. And so it is. Thank you."*

Anytime you catch yourself feeling powerless or victimized, then strengthen the belief that you are the creator of your reality. No matter what is happening, how you are being treated, or how powerless you feel to change certain aspects in your life, you do have the authority. You have a choice and this is what you are choosing. Even though you cannot imagine how you would be choosing what you are experiencing. Telling yourself this will help you take responsibility in understanding that you are the creator of your life. Take time to recognize the decisions you made that created the situation you are in. You do not need others to give you what you want. You and your higher self can create any life you dream of. The power of the mind can paint these wonders and bring it to fruition. Having one negative thought will negate and block it from happening. Quickly tell your Spirit team to cancel the negative thought you had and replace it with a positive affirmation. Keep your vibrational energy high!

Avoid getting caught up in depressing feelings surrounding where you're currently at. There are positives to every situation. If you're feeling dispirited, then look at the hidden blessings in your current reality. Okay, so you are not happy at your job and you want to leave or move into a position within the company that has more meaning to you. Change your thought vibrations to highlight something positive. For example, feel thankful that you have a job to begin with, and that your bills are paid. By shifting the vibration of your thoughts into something optimistic, you invite that energy in! It will not be long before you do get the job, career, relationship, or home you want. After shifting your thoughts into something positive, then take little action steps towards making your dream happen.

It is not enough to remain optimistic and positive. This is a vital aspect, yes, but you must also pay attention to your Spirit team's messages and guidance intended to lead you to your ultimate goal. You need to take the action steps they put in front of you in order to create a dent towards your dream. Investigate and research the areas of your interest, then dive on in. When you are healthy and clear minded, then you raise your vibration. Raising your vibration opens up the channels of communication to your Spirit team on the other side. They show you the next steps by handing you little opportunities that propel you one move closer to your dream. When you are dispirited, then you do not notice the messages of assistance. Be happy and optimistic in believing that you have everything you want now. This positive view opens your world right up. Many of the Archangels can assist you with this. Call upon Archangel Raphael to elevate your mood when it takes a dip into pessimism. Call on Archangel Michael when you're experiencing fear. Call on Archangel Raziel to assist you in manifesting your dreams.

Chapter Seven

DISCONNECTING AND ELIMINATING

Are you putting more focus and attention into your professional life leaving your personal life neglected? If one area in your life gets more attention than the other, then you have created an imbalance. When this happens, you are more inclined to remain stressed out, tired, and irritable. My Spirit team emphasizes on keeping your life in balance. Do this by honing in on the two most popular areas of your life: Home and work. This is the personal and professional.

Disconnect from the world as often as possible to clear your mind. Running your body into overdrive causes an array of health issues that are not limited to daily burn out. Disconnecting from your computer and phone for a few hours at a time is a great way to start. An even better way if possible is doing this for an entire day at least once a week. Use that time to interact with yourself or a close one such as a friend, your family or relationship partner. Hanging out with someone who is negative, toxic or feeds an addiction is not using the disconnection wisely. If you are going to use the disconnection time to put in quality time with a loved one, ensure that it is someone who is optimistic, joyful and makes healthy life choices.

Avoid bringing your work home, or your personal life to work. You manage your soul and body. Only you know what area in your life is lopsided or receives little to no attention. Take charge and personally manage your day. If you are working too much, then take some vacation time off, even if it is a day or two a month. Focusing heavily on your interpersonal relationships and home life causes strain. Find a hobby or activity you enjoy doing that is productive. Make sure you keep your home and work life balanced otherwise you will experience symptoms of burn out.

STAY AWAY FROM NOISE

I do not pay much attention to the news, media and gossip sites. It is typically days after a major story has hit the news when I hear about it through the grapevine. By this time, it has already been going on awhile. I discover that the world is in an uproar over something ridiculous or gossipy. I say ridiculous because all is always well. No one truly cares about the story since it's not long before they've shifted their focus onto the next attention grabbing headline. The uproars and the lynch mob mentality behavior are products of human ego. They serve no one and benefit nothing. All it does is add negativity and suppressed, blocked energy onto the planet. Human ego loves to create drama and issues out of a story. This goes for those that soak themselves into a story reacting to it negatively in some manner. Other responsible parties are those who work in the media feeding it to the masses like poison. The stories have a design intended to get a rise out of you and work you up into a panicked or angry frenzy. When in the end, everything works itself out the way it's intended. There will always be something new in the media that pops up to suddenly divert everybody's focus onto the latest scandal, end of the world talk, or court trial. Yet they have ironically forgotten all about what they were upset about a week before that had meant so much to them at the time. How do so many live their lives donating so much of their energy into useless noise? There is no point to that existence. This exhausts your energy and keeps you from doing something that benefits you, the planet, and its people in a positive way. Stay away from all of it and focus on what makes your heart sing and brings you or others joy.

If you notice that you are feeling agitated, then the best thing to do is to make immediate soul enhancement steps. Think of what relaxes you or brings you joy. Head immediately to your nearest nature locale where there is little to no people. Breathe in all of that beautiful nature, the trees, grass, flowers, and ask God to surround you with angels creating a healing love cushion. Ask that they extract any negative ions that have latched onto your loving spirit.

If your days have been particularly intense, you may say something like this: *"Dear God. Please surround me with a hundred angels today creating a cushion of love. Thank you."*

When I have said those words on a particularly severe day in the past, I would find that my day would alter from intense to breezing effortlessly through it afterwards.

Are you procrastinating? Are you feeling like you are running around in a circle heading nowhere? This is a clue that it is time to work on breaking away from the self-imposed prison you have constructed for yourself. Break away from running around in a circle and find another path to go down. Break away from anything that is holding you back from moving forward. You may need to go back and re-examine what it is you want and how it is you are going about in obtaining it. Look at what needs modifying in your life. Take that new enlightened information and run with it. Shine a light on specific areas in your life that you are not paying attention to that need some revisions. Those adjustments will lead you towards the Sun and the happiness you crave.

CHECKING AN EX-LOVER'S PAGE

More people than not have admitted to spying on their ex-lover's social media page. If you're obsessing over an ex-lover who is no longer with you in your life on a daily basis for months and beyond, then this is a block which lowers your vibration. This ex has left you, moved on, or perhaps blocked you on social media, email, phone or phone app with no explanation. Yet, you cannot find a way to let it go and move on. It's a natural reaction to feel immediate hurt, but the goal is to move past this upset over the breakup or separation. You will not be able to if you wonder about them indefinitely to the point where it puts you in a funk. This negative state lowers your vibration. If you're in this state everyday for a year, imagine how stuck that might make you feel. That is until you move swiftly through the negative circumstance by making important life changes and adjustments to reach a place where you're content again. Somebody who is not a part of your life anymore is no longer your higher self's priority or interest.

You might find that you are checking their social media pages from time to time to see what they're up to. You're looking for signs that they might be interested in you again or perhaps you want to see who are they talking to. How about what photos they post online with other people in them? Could they be romantically or sexually connected to any of the people in the photo? What about those who comment on your ex's page? This is an example of your ego desperately curious to know or find out some clues about what's going on with this ex lover. This lowers your vibration and creates a block in your life. There are no exceptions to this. If someone is no longer interested in communicating with you, then that is your cue to work on moving on. If you feel there is still a connection with them, then message them how you feel once. If they have blocked you, or they do not respond to your message, then that is your answer to begin the process of continuing on with your life without them.

The moment you go to this person's social media page to read their posts in order to find out "information", then your vibration drops. A low vibration is what is a result of being depressed, miserable or angry and agitated. When you focus heavily on this ex, talking about them, focusing on them, and wondering about it, then this drops your vibration. Your vibration continues to drop every time you obsess over their every move. One sign you are not over them is that every time you read their posts you experience some form of upset, distress or uneasy feeling. After a year of this you might find that it has ultimately destroyed your life force, work, friendships, soul and creative life among other things. It stalls your forward movement, until you begin the process of re-raising your vibration again and getting back to that place of perfect contentment. And you will get there with effort and discipline. It's a steady process as you deal with the death of what no longer is in your life to make room for what is. Your interest in the coming and going's of others will decline and you'll notice improvement and positive changes happening gradually as a result.

FULL MOON RELEASING

Release that which has been delaying you and holding you back from positive progress. You likely already know what you need to let go of, but are procrastinating out of fear or indecision. It is anything or anyone that brings you down or prompts you to experience consistent inadequate feelings such as depression, anger or stress. This also includes foods and substances that are not good for you and cause your body to react negatively such as giving you low energy or irritability. This delays you from taking positive action and in moving forward. Release anything negative so that you can truly be free and soar upwards to where your higher self lives. When you release negative stuff, then you are on your way to obtaining your dreams. Your dreams come true as a result of this release, but you have to do the work. You have to release negative thoughts, patterns, lifestyle choices and people.

The Full Moon transit which happens once a month is a great time for releasing, re-aligning and then manifesting (positively - so watch your thoughts!) Many use the night of the Full Moon to release that which no longer serves them or their higher self. Release anything or anyone that you know is toxic and causes you to experience uncomfortable feelings. The energy of the Full Moon is potent, intense, and powerful. It brings up all sorts of feelings and thoughts. It has the power to magnify and direct your energy in large ways. This is why it is important to be crystal-clear with your thoughts in general, and especially on the night of the Full Moon.

Simply having intention can make this release happen efficiently. One way is by meditating or gazing upon the Full Moon for 5-15 minutes. Take a deep breath in, exhale, and repeat until you are fully relaxed. Breathe in and connect with the Moon so that you are one with it. You can do this longer than 15 minutes if you choose. Sitting underneath the Full Moon outside in order to make contact with you is even better. Sometimes this is not realistic if it is a cloudy or rainy night, but as long as the intention is there is all that matters. Mentally visualize what you would like to remove from your life. Follow that with what you would like to see come to fruition. This brings in your Spirit team by your side notating the work you are putting in to make healthy life changes. Archangel Haniel is the hierarchy angel who you can benefit from working with. Ask her to be with you through this Full Moon releasing process. She awakens your third eye chakra which opens up clairvoyance.

FLOWERS

Flowers raise your vibration, so fill your surroundings with flowers. Purchase flowers or put up photographs of flowers. Having the real thing is the most beneficial. If the only option is a framed picture of a flower due to severe allergies or other circumstances, then that is better than no flowers. If you have allergies, call on Archangel Raphael and ask him to reduce or eliminate the severity of the allergies. Pay attention to the guidance he places in your path where other alternatives to having a flower can come into play.

Lean into the flower and breathe it in. If this is a photograph of a flower, then envision that it is real as you lean in to breathe it in. Notice how wide open the flower is with its arms outstretched. Take it all in allowing it to awaken and open up your mind and senses. Meditate on the flower or image and take a deep breath in. On the exhale release any negative thoughts or lower vibration words that you have been using. The flower's arms expand wide giving you a big hug.

The flowers, trees, grass and all of nature are gifts from God to help you relax and connect with your Spirit team. God created flowers for numerous purposes. One of them is to surround you with beauty. Beauty and flowers both raise your vibration. It's a double whammy! It is not okay to destroy nature and this world through greed and naivety. Flowers keep this planet alive and to keep you feeling alive. Flowers are little reminders of the beauty that exists in the Spirit world, which is abundantly ripe with flowers. Nature is a powerful sense awakener with immense healing properties. When you take in a huge inhale of a flower, you feel invigorated. Your mind opens up becoming clear, focused and stimulated. Absorbing nature regularly prompts you to experience the natural uplifting feelings of well-being.

Placing flowers around you can invite positive circumstances into your life. Each color tends to bring in specific energy into your vicinity. The darker the shade of that particular color, then the more intense it will be. The lighter the shade of that color, then the softer the energy will be. If it is a pink flower, it can bring in more love into your life. If that pink is a deeper rose color, then the love will be heavier, more intense. The lighter the pink is in that flower, then the softer the love is or subtle it is.

Here is an example cheat sheet of the healing properties that the color of a flower can give off. Place these flowers around your space if you would like to invite in a higher energy for a specific desire:

- ❖ **Red** – passion, romance, sexiness, deep relationships and commitments
- ❖ **Pink** – Love, beauty, attractiveness
- ❖ **Yellow** – Joy, optimism, success, ideas, thoughts, friendships
- ❖ **Green** – Healing, releasing, cleansing
- ❖ **Violet** – Spiritual awakenings, protection, third eye opening
- ❖ **White** – Harmony, Purity, vibration lifting, hope
- ❖ **Orange** – Growth, empowerment, expansiveness, career
- ❖ **Blue** – Strength, courage, calming, honor, creativity

There are books available on the market devoted to flowers that can offer more detail and insight into the healing properties that exist. Do an Internet search and type in something like: 'flower therapy'.

YOUR LIGHT IS POWER

Show your best self by sharing your light with others on a daily basis. Let it out and let it shine bright. This inspires a mighty movement of peace. The hardness and toxicity that has plagued humankind for so long is outdated. The light exists inside of you. You must allow it to take back the control of your surroundings. Be a warrior of light. Do your best to stay in that space even when you stumble upon a roadblock or a difficult human soul. Demanding people are merely acting out from their ego, which has no power or validity with anything real or long lasting.

The ego lives in fear and acts out in fits of temper much like a child having an outburst when it doesn't get what it wants. You find peace, joy, strength and love when you remain centered in the light. When you lose your way, ask for heavenly assistance to get back on track. The more you ask for help and work with your Spirit team to reach this space of contentment, then the easier it gets. What can work for you might be lighting a candle and meditating on this light. Call in your Spirit team to begin the process of re-aligning your soul. Empty out your negative thoughts as you focus on this candlelight. Close your eyes and envision that the flame of the light is taking over any negative thoughts and blasting it away while lifting it off your body. Make room in your consciousness to receive the messages coming in from Spirit to help you be at peace and feel encompassed by love.

I have crossed paths with a wide variety of people who have different belief systems and values. I have witnessed those who might disagree with any of this or who find it to be ineffective. Yet, these are the same people that struggle in a constant uphill battle. Or they might be the ones who have been stagnant with no hope for escape. When in those states, your ego dominates your life big time ensuring that you never progress. Within you is the knowledge of all lifetimes. Within you is the knowledge of why you are here. Pay attention to your intuition as that is one of the many barometer gauges that exist within your soul that accurately receives heavenly messages. All human souls receive heavenly communication everyday without exception. It is irrelevant what the soul's personal values and beliefs are, and whether they're aware that it is indeed their Guides and Angels. Pay attention to the messages in order to help you navigate through life much easier than if you were not aware of them.

Keeping your vibration high takes daily work. It's a lifestyle and view change you're adopting. One day you are riding on cloud nine with joy, which raises your vibration. Your vibration remains high until a negative thought enters your mind thus causing it to take a tip again. The next day you go on a drinking binge. This drinking binge prompts your vibration to drop astronomically. It can be a struggle to raise it than it is to drop it. Raising it back up can feel like pushing a huge boulder up a steep hill. Those privy to this knowledge can raise their vibration much easier than someone unaware of what to do in order to get it there. Having an interfering culprit like the ego is what gets its kicks out of double-crossing you and ensuring your vibration stays low. It makes sure that you do not succeed. When you make a commitment to incorporating higher vibration methods into your life every day, then you will notice the changes in your life shifting in a more positive direction.

Chapter Eight

THE POWER OF THE MIND

It is true that having the great relationship, career and home will not necessarily make you happy, but you might likely be happier. It's a human need to desire the basic materialistic necessities in this Earthly life. It's important to remember that genuine contentment comes from within. Focus on adjusting any ongoing upsetting feelings and thoughts inside you and then work your way out. Unsettling feelings are the ego mind creating something out of nothing. It restricts you from moving forward. You have the authority to free yourself of the prison that is formed by the power of your mind. Both your higher self and lower self are in constant struggle over who is to be the driver of your life. Often times your lower self or ego insists on dominating. It dictates and instructs you on how you will feel or react to something.

If your mind can create this restriction, then it has the power to undo it. The power of the mind can cause you unnecessary harm, but it can just as easily break the heavy chains that latch onto your soul. Your mind digs these holes to bury you in and stop you from progressing. It will do this by prompting you to reach for addictions and time wasters. It will do its best to lower your energy and mood. The false reality your lower self creates has the intention of stopping you from experiencing joy. Ignore that voice and choose to be free! Re-center and align your mind by taking some quiet time out. Do this preferably in nature where Spirits power is heavy and therefore the healing qualities more powerful. Avoid choosing to needlessly suffer. Wrestle your inner ego demon to the ground. Decide to stand in the power of your high and most magnificent self.

Why does it sometimes feel like a job to get happy? Your thoughts can either cause damage or bring in magical manifestations to you. Which would you like to have? The irony we notice is that it feels so easy for you to think about the things that you're upset about. Instead think about the things you appreciate and love more often. When you're angry or negatively critical, then this adds unnecessary burdens to your aura. Your ego passes it around to those around you bringing them down in the process. They do the same and so forth. You notice how unsafe this makes the planet as it creates an endless pay it forward domino effect.

This dangerous energy that comes from your

thoughts expands destroying anything in its wake. You do this by running into other souls and complaining to them. You call up your friends or run into a close colleague and gossip about the negative happenings in your day and life. There is so much energy invested in placing hyper attention on the negative circumstances that you perceive to be throughout each day. The additional danger is that nothing good comes of it. Not only does it darken and lower your spirit vibration, but it also brings more of that negative stuff to you. You are manifesting that which you don't want simply by talking and thinking about it. You can be an innocent soul who puts in the work to keep their vibration high, but by watching or reading any negative media force fed upon you will lower your vibration.

Think happy thoughts, feel grateful, appreciative, and move into the zone of inner stillness. Your vibration will rise and you will manifest at higher levels. Suddenly you will notice everything going right. It's one good thing after another. For instance, you receive a check in the mail you weren't expecting. This is followed by obtaining a job you were dreaming about. You head on outside and take a walk basking in the wonders of your higher self and run smack into your new love soul mate. This soul mate is experiencing the same vibrational rush too since like attracts like.

One soul is plagued with negative thoughts and is terribly unhappy experiencing one hindrance after another. This person finds sudden aches and pains in their physical body that doesn't seem to go away. They're late for work, get a flat tire, and their love partner breaks up with them. This is all in the same week!

You have the power to bring in anything you desire through the positive utilization of your mind. The gifts of manifestation live within you. It starts with your thoughts. You have free will choice to choose how you are going to use those thoughts. This is followed by your feelings. When your thoughts and feelings are balanced, aligned, and radiating with optimism on an equal level, then positive circumstances enter your life. When your thoughts and feelings are negative, then the opposite effects take place.

You might say, "That person I'm attracted to and desire will never be attracted to someone like me. And I'll never get that job."
What do you think you're going to get out of that thinking process? No love mate and no job.

It is understood that as a human soul something will throw your day off. It will spiral you into a negative mood. The challenge is then to be conscious of this when it happens and pull right back out of that before those negative thoughts cause additional catastrophic events to happen. The real reality of what you are experiencing at that very moment that has thrown your life for a loop has no basis for being. It is not real in the way that your higher self and soul know it. You are here in a physical body at this time, but eventually that body will be no longer. The things you fret over cease to exist and yet your attitude still sticks until you realize the truth. Just because others have said that this is the way it must be, does not make it true. This is their reality and the one they choose to live in. If someone is unhappy with you because of who you are and the way you choose to live your life, then the odds are that they are unhappy with everyone and everything around them. This is not your soul's concern to fret over someone else's challenges by making it your own.

Chasing physical interests only pushes it that much further away from you. Those who have an understanding of certain spiritual practices may find from time to time that when things go wrong, they might affirm positive words in a harsh angry manner. "I am happy! I have everything I want! I love life!" You are saying it fuming and irritated. The vibration that is being directed out into the ethers is an angry and irate vibration. The energy darted out is the feeling and your intent. When you feel this angry, it is best not to state anything at all until you've relaxed and calmed down a bit. Cry out for assistance to your Spirit team of Guides and Angels, or whomever you feel most comfortable with. You can cry out: "Angels! Help!" You are immediately heard. If you're going to cry anything out in anger, then scream out for heavenly assistance, since that's the positive help that will be forthcoming. You may need to have patience for any intervention, but have faith that you are indeed heard and help is on its way. This is far more efficient than immediately crying out positive word affirmations in an angry manner. Since it is the tone and feeling behind them that resonate with the universe.

When you are angry or upset, give yourself permission to have a time out and sit alone away from others. Allow the angels to lift the negative thoughts and ugliness off your body. Visualize these eons being lifted high off your body and soul until they are nowhere near you. Take deep breathes in and exhale out any negativity and ugliness. Find a space of contentment and allow it room for your positive manifestations to take flight.

Someone who displays high vibrational traits is a happy person. They feel immense joy and this is outwardly directed. They're optimistic and kind, which is not to be mistaken for weakness. On the contrary, they are strong, yet diplomatic and compassionate. They're calm and peaceful people who show love to others. They guard themselves from harsher energies that might surround them. God gave human souls an ego and free will to act how they please even if it sinks their spirit and lowers their vibration. It is up to the individual soul to discover that the way they've been operating has not been successful.

Communicating with your team of Guides and Angels is praying to God. The billions of prayers that come from human souls look like varying shades and sizes of lights being shot into the ethers. Clairvoyantly it may look like magical white light finger painting. When angels see the lights that come out of human souls during a prayer or affirmation, they see their true higher self banging around somewhere in that dense body they inhabit.

It doesn't matter if you're an atheist, or if you

believe in God or whatever your beliefs are. It doesn't matter if you call it a prayer, or a positive affirmation or just a thought. It doesn't matter if you don't believe in any of it. Heaven has heard you the second a thought has entered your mind. You have put it out into the universe. Your thoughts are prayers and affirmations. All thoughts are heard including the good and the bad. Regardless of the nature of the thought, you will likely get it. The response to your request is matched to the vibration of the prayer or affirmation you are putting out into the universe. There is no set time frame on when your desire comes to fruition. You may get it tomorrow or in six months. If you believe in obtaining something with powerful intention, then you are heard. The stronger your intention is, and the good nature of this intention, the more likely it will come to fruition.

The rays of light darting out from individual souls are in varying shades of light and sizes due to the intention and vibration of that prayer. If someone is praying or saying a positive affirmation, but yet there is no feeling behind it, then the light being shot out is dim. You are heard, but the way the prayers and affirmations are answered is much like an assembly line. Say your request with positive, uplifting feeling behind it. It's possible you've grown frustrated and this energy vibration is picked up on in your prayer. Seeing no movement has caused your faith to be shaken over time. The tone behind your prayer or affirmation appears weak. The light of that prayer and affirmation is not seen as strong as others.

In the past, when I've cried out in frustration or anger demanding assistance with something, I miraculously see it come to fruition. The angels do not see your ego stomping around in a fury, but rather your intention. The reason my desire came to realization was it was seen that I wanted it with all of my heart and soul. The energy of the desire is so great that it was matched and returned right back to me.

New born souls in a human body are left at the mercy with those older than them who do not always know any better. An adult can deal with life's repercussions better than a human child. A mother, father, parent, or guardian's prayer request for help with their child is therefore heard first. Sometimes caring for a child that needs assistance beyond what a human soul can help with results in a cry out for help. This is heard and responded to sooner than later. The bottom line is to watch the nature of your thoughts, feelings, affirmations and prayers. If you feel your faith is waning, or you're reaching the boiling point of throwing in the towel, ask Heaven to boost your faith and patience. Continue to ask daily if you're not seeing any movement. Some people ask for help once and then weeks later will say, "Well I asked, but nothing happened." It's important to continue to put that positive energy vibration out there regularly. You're also developing a connection with your Spirit team in Heaven. This is rather than only contacting them when you want help or need something.

When I've asked for heavenly assistance, I always get it. Sometimes it's right away and other times it's eventually down the line. I found through experimenting with prayers my entire life that they do help. After you've requested help, you must pay attention to the signs that are being given. When you're bathed in negative emotions, then that blocks your clarity from seeing how the assistance is coming. Express gratitude along with your desires. It's important to include appreciation with your communications with Heaven. Whenever I head down to the beach near where I live, I say blessings and gratitude. I do this silently every time I'm there. I do not take the gifts handed to me for granted.

Sometimes the answers you're looking for come in ways that you do not expect them to. Other times there is a delay as Heaven maneuvers certain pieces of the puzzle before what's needed to know is revealed. There are also the experiences you have to endure in order to reach enlightenment on your own. Never give up communicating with your Spirit team and God. Have patience and faith that the answers will be forthcoming even if it's not on that given day.

Chapter Nine

FIND THE LOVE WITHIN

When you're faced with circumstances that do not jive with your higher self, examine how you arrived at that place. Look at the underlying cause that has prompted you to feel negative when this happens. Identify it, and then dig deep into understanding why it has upset you. There are circumstances that no doubt have made you angry or prompted feelings of discomfort. Maybe you ran into someone at the store who was rude to you. You being a sensitive absorbed that like nobody's business. It ends up putting you in a funk. For some sensitive's, they'll be angry for a minute, others for hours, or you could be one of those who immerses in the energy for the rest of the day. Avoid beating yourself up over it. It just means that you're a hyper sensitive psychic sponge. You have compassion and love within you as all souls do, even though this might be difficult to grasp. Whenever you witness ugliness in someone else, remember that they were born with the deepest love and compassion beyond measure. What you're observing with them is the darkness of ego at its best. This soul has given its power away to their lower self and ego. The ego cannot be reasoned with or convinced of anything, but of what it wants. The ego seeks to sabotage themselves or others. It can be someone who slanders a product they did not care for. A high vibrational soul who is not pleased with something does not waste it's time resorting to negativity or in giving it any attention. It only focuses on the products it enjoyed.

When you witness aggression or disrespectful behavior flying at you, then you will absorb that energy. It seeps into your aura and soul. It causes an array of negative circumstances and moods to assault you. What is important is that you find positive exercises that can assist you in releasing it and letting that go. It might feel easier said than done, but when a slight happens in your world, your ego has trouble letting go of it. When you understand this concept of separating yourself from the troublesome ego, it becomes simpler to manage and temper it.

When you have a higher degree of sensitivity than other souls, then you are more likely to be affected by someone else's ego. You're a psychic sponge who easily absorbs the negative or off putting energies in others. It is a gift, but at times it can feel like a curse when you enter environments with human souls displaying low vibrational behavioral patterns. You absorb that negative energy which drops your mood affecting your inner and outer world.

When you grow negative, moody, or agitated, then this is a sign of two possible conclusions. One is that you've ingested low a vibrational food or drink. Or you may have absorbed this energy from someone toxic you crossed paths with.

It can even be a stranger on the sidewalk who walked passed you. If they're displaying low vibrational behavior, then that energy is lodged in their aura. As a tuned in sensitive psychic sponge, you've absorbed that into your aura sometimes without knowing it. Although, the super tuned in psychic sponges are typically aware they just absorbed this energy from someone in passing.

The souls you absorbed this energy from do not always intend to have a low vibration. It's usually done innocently and naively, or sometimes in other words, not knowing any better. Some souls have not evolved enough to be more in tune to something outside of themselves. This is partially why that particular soul is living an Earthly life.

Those in tune with the other side, the soul and spirit, are turned off by harsh people and energies. They steer clear of those who perpetually display low vibrational traits.

This coldness and reserve has grown in others thanks to the technological age. Newer and future generations are being raised on devices that train you to be lacking in honest face-to-face soul connections. For those that have gone out on a date, you've probably noticed some of the typical preliminary questions. They want to know what your job is or what kind of work do you do. What kind of car do you drive? These ego driven questions are externally based. Your job does not define you in real reality, but the human ego has set their life up in a way that their whole world revolves around what kind of job you do. Who cares what you do for a living. Unless you're working in a field that is your passion and it brings you joy, then it is irrelevant what kind of work you do. This passion is your life purpose, but many do not work in jobs that are their passion. For most, it is a paycheck that squeezes the life force out of that soul. They're usually under stress and grumbling about life in general.

When you absorb the ions of negative and cold energy around you, then this can put a damper on your spirit until you address it. You can sit around and hope that something amazing will happen around you that suddenly raises your vibration, or you can address it and do something about it immediately.

Detaching and releasing this energy is easier than one might believe. It can be going for a walk in a nature setting. This is followed by taking deep healthy breathes in and requesting that your spirit team release any and all negative energy that has latched onto your soul. It can be getting together with an optimistic friend who observes healthy life choices, or someone who always lifts your aura just by being in your vicinity. You can throw on a funny movie or make love to your relationship partner. What you're trying to do is re-raise your vibration. Taking basic soul enhancing steps when an assault has attacked your aura can do the trick.

A Vibration Raising Exercise

Everyone has experienced some hard times at one time or another. You have negative things to say about it. The ego fixates on the horrid that came out of that. Rise above your ego and ask yourself, "What greatness did I get out of that experience? What was awesome about it?"

The soul's experiences happen for a reason regardless if they're challenging or not. It is not because you did something to deserve it, but because your soul is destined for greatness. You're here in this Earthly life school to find ways that suit you in order to enhance your soul and spirit. You're not here to find out the latest sale on jeans or rip through relationships selfishly with no care in the world. In order to improve, you have much to gain. When something negative happens in your world, work on looking at it from an optimistic perspective.

An exercise you can do is to pick up a journal or a notebook. Use that notepad as your diary to put in only optimistic viewpoints in your life. When you find that you're buried heavily in negative thoughts and emotions unable to break away, take a moment to pull the notebook out. Devote a page or more to whatever it is that is upsetting you. If it's a person, then write that person's name in your journal entry. Instead of focusing on what they did to upset you or whatever circumstance has upset you, shift that into something positive. Think about all of the qualities you love about the person that has angered you. Remove your ego from the equation and look at that person through the eyes of an egoless angel. List everything that is positive about them and how that affects you in an optimistic way. I know some may grumble when reading that, and believe me I understand. I have an ego too! When someone has hurt or angered you, of course it's going to be difficult to see them through the eyes of love. Know that when you're looking at them through the eyes of love, you're not condoning their behavior and nor do you have to remain best friends with them. You're doing this exercise as a release. It's for your benefit in order to remove that old, tired, angry energy you're carrying around that surrounds the person or circumstance. You do not need that energy, but in order to release it, acknowledging it with love is what raises your vibration. When your vibration is raised you are more apt to receiving clearer communication from the spirit world, which in turn assists you on your path towards abundance in all forms.

Your mind may begin to wander to all of the things you feel this person has done that has hurt or upset you. However, you will not write those things down. Remember this is a positive journal. You will immediately adjust your thoughts back to the positive things about this person. Let's say it was an ex-lover who cheated on you, was abusive, or left you and the relationship. You will not write any of those things down, but rather will focus on their good qualities. If you're only able to come up with one good quality, then write that one down. It is an exercise that takes much effort in this case, because you're holding anger towards this person for doing one or all of the things I suggested. Your ego refuses to see the goodness in someone who has upset or hurt you.

If it is a circumstance that happened to cause you upset, then you will write down in this journal the optimistic features that have come out of that. For example, you receive a traffic ticket. Instead of focusing heavily on how you have no time to take care of the ticket, or no money to pay for it, write down the positive benefits that you've gained from the ticket. You might write something down like: "This has taught me to drive more carefully." That statement feels far better than saying, "I have no money. How am I going to pay for this! It wasn't even my fault!"

This exercise may not immediately change your life, but it will gradually guide you into positively changing your life. It will assist you in getting into the habit of bouncing back from upsetting situations much more quickly. It will help you to view circumstances and people in a more positive light. The key is if you're going to play this game, then you have to play objectively. Putting all things positive and optimistic in this journal is the exercise. Only write your blessings, appreciations and gratitude for situations and people in your life. This absolutely includes everything and everyone that causes you to feel negative emotions. This might be challenging, but in the end it will be rewarding as you are re-training your mind to think positively. This raises your vibration in the process, which assists with attracting in positive circumstances and people to you over the course of time. Because it raises your vibration, it also clears out the debris that accumulates in and around the communication line to Heaven and your Spirit team. If it doesn't do anything, but allow you to start shining your true loving light, then that is all that matters in the end.

The ego is a wretched problem seeker. It might appear to be louder than your higher self and your Spirit team of guides and angels. This is due to a couple of factors. The atmosphere of the Earth plane is extremely thick and dense that connecting to the other side through all of the toxic debris makes it challenging. Your guides and angels are louder and more powerful than any ego. Yet, when the soul is in the Earth dimension, the communication lines are heavier and dirtier. The ego rises through the dirt. It already rises as soon as your soul enters into this human life. The ego is activated in a big way. When the soul is in the earth plane it's like roaming through life with ear plugs on. Anyone who has put ear plugs on to sleep at night may point out how they can sometimes faintly hear light sounds with them on. The higher self strains to hear Heaven through this muffled sound. When a human soul lives in a higher vibrational state, this allows light in, which gives rise to the higher self. Suddenly that soul is hearing their guides and angels more clearly than usual.

You are not alone as you are surrounded by at least one Spirit Guide and one Guardian Angel from your human birth until human death. They assist you down the right path in order to fulfill your purpose while here. When you are in your higher self's state you connect with your Spirit team on the other side with greater efficiency. When you are in your lower self's state or ego, then you block heavenly guidance and messages that keep you on the right path and assist you in achieving your desires. In my connections with Heaven, I've discovered that all are loved and seen through the eyes of love. Do your best to keep the darkness of your ego in check and exude love full time!

Chapter Ten

PATH TO ABUNDANCE

It's true that having the great relationship, career, home and car won't necessarily make you happy, but you may likely be happier. It's a human need to desire the basic necessities of life. However, a great many people who obtain these things still protest to not feeling happy and satisfied afterwards. I run in many circles that include those who are obscenely wealthy, as well as friends and acquaintances that are well known publicly due to my previous work in the entertainment business. I can tell you their problems are not any less important than anybody else's. They have money, a great career and popularity, sure, but they still have internal personal issues they are battling that have to be addressed. They have endless flowing money and are not completely content. This is because true happiness comes from within. You start there and then work your way externally. When you are experiencing joy and contentment inside, then the other needs manifest more quickly.

The fine print needs to be stated because often in some spiritual contexts it is taught that happiness comes from within and that craving a great relationship or career will not make you happy. If you are always feeling miserable and then you obtain the great career, it may still leave you feeling empty, but it could possibly offer you added fulfillment that will elevate your vibration. If you're miserable, it is highly unlikely you would attract and obtain a great relationship or career to begin with anyway. A wonderful fulfilling love relationship will enhance your life that is already enhanced. Bottom line is find that space within you that helps you to feel satisfied now, and then the rest will follow. The abundance of wealth, love and home will be an added bonus that enriches your life even more. You are then able to put more focus on others, help those in need, and change things that need shifting in this world. When you are lavished in abundance, you are in a brighter mind space to focus on your life purpose without the added need of personal worries like paying your bills or finding a love relationship.

The key to abundance is feeling it before you see it. You feel it by believing it. It's in the way that you think and function. You can get there by saying affirmations to yourself daily until its part of your life and part of your soul. I am exhilarated. I am love. I am joy. I am in a place of perfect contentment. All my needs are met. All my desires are met. I sit back in awe at the wonders around me. I am taken care of in all ways. I have no needs because what I require as a human soul flows to me effortlessly. Abundance flows to me like water. I don't need it, but it is there and keeps on coming. I feel bliss. I am uplifted. I am always laughing. I am always seeing the humor around me. What I need is here with me now. I sit in peace and notice the abundance and love flow to me and around me like a spinning wheel. The more content I am, then the more the abundance flows. When I am resistant I am not there. When I am emotional I am not there. When I stand strong in confidence I am there. When I am sure of myself I am there. When I give love I am there. When I allow myself to receive love I am there. When I have compassion I am there.

These are examples of the thoughts that need to dominate your less than stellar thoughts in order to bring more abundance to you.

Let's say you were laid off from your job and you want to pursue the career of your dreams in opening up an art gallery. You know this will cost at least twenty grand in a good area. The devastation of being laid off from one's job depending on the scenario can be a blessing in disguise. It's a great sign to take you out of your comfort zone. It's understood about the ramifications that come out of being laid off or leaving a job in any form. The angels also understand that as human souls we have to survive, we have groceries to pick up and we have bills to pay. The flip side is that it's almost a blessing in disguise giving you the freedom to choose what you are going to do next. Going after work that is your passion takes some orchestrating and maneuvering.

When I was sixteen I knew I would be writing books. I knew that I wouldn't start writing books out of the gate. I decided to first look for a job where I could incorporate creativity, writing and storytelling. The entertainment business came to mind and I went on a huge hunt and fight to get in. When I turned twenty-three years old, I was hired by one of the top box office actresses at the time to read scripts and write coverage on it for her production company. It had the best of all worlds I was looking for to incorporate writing in some way. I was doing some writing work while getting paid. This led to the next thing and all great things came down from that.

If you wanted to open your art gallery, then consider pursuing obtaining a job in an art gallery. You're not going to start your own studio tomorrow, but perhaps look for work that is somehow connected to that world and genre so that you're inside. Accepting work as an assistant in an art gallery puts you in the arena of your interest. Be the receptionist if it gets you into that world. Take whatever work position you need to take that gets you in the door of the genre that is your interest and the rest will follow.

We're all teachers and have much to learn from one another. Everyone is important. Everyone has the ability to communicate with Heaven, God, Archangels, Saints and Angels and so on. No one is more special than anybody else in that regard. Wise Ones help others improve themselves and their life by having a crystal clear communication with the other side. The main messages are of joy, peace and happiness. Prepare to make leaps of change that you desire. Transformations are positive and life changing. It's like the caterpillar changing into the butterfly and freed from its prison on the ground. It soars out of its protective skin to greater heights. Happiness and contentment comes with change even if the change is unwanted initially. Everything is well in the end.

Abundance Exercise

Sit or stand in a stance of perfect contentment. You can do this anywhere. Sit or stand in front of a burning candlelight, or in a nature setting. Light some incense and play some soft music if you're at home. Take several deep-exhaling breaths. Recite affirmations surrounding any areas of blocks you'd like to release from your aura. You can say something like:

1. I wish to release any blockages within and around me.

2. I wish to release any blockages preventing me from achieving success.

3. I wish to release any blockages preventing me from obtaining that great love relationship.

Stand or sit with your legs slightly apart. Spread your arms out slightly apart. Cup your hands together as if you have a bird sitting in it. Lift your hands into the air as they're cupped together and say:

"I accept abundance from the universe gracefully and without fear or guilt of receiving. I am deserving of the incoming gifts of abundance."

Exercise and Nutrition Tips

Some of the many messages from the other side are repetitive. The reason is they want everyone working at optimum levels. This is not for their benefit, but for yours. They know you will be happier and more at peace when you are radiating high vibrational energy. There are times when I have had to struggle to remember adhering to some of their wisdom. As disciplined as I am, I still have a human ego that gets in my own way once in awhile. No one is perfect and nor is Heaven expecting or asking for perfection. They do however know what your soul desires. They know what steps will help you get there. You do the best you can.

The more passion and dedication you have to make positive improvements in your life, then the closer you will be to achieving abundance. Exercise is a key factor in whipping your entire state of mind, body and soul into shape. Your soul feels weighted down when your body is not functioning properly. This happens when you do not take care of it. Be sure to get regular bouts of exercise for at least fifteen minutes a day. The more the better, but starting low and working your way up is an easy way to make the transition. Turn on your music player and get into it. Music raises your vibration and uplifts your spirit closer to God so crank it up!

Eating fresh fruit and vegetables are another of the many ways to raise your vibration. Make the pact to care about your body and soul.

Juicing some of your fruits and vegetables helps the nutrients absorb into your body much more readily. Juicing contributes to keeping your body in shape, while cleansing your organs and adding increased energy levels. This gives you more power and energy during the day to put towards being productive. You have more quality time to spend with friends and family or any other healthy pursuits. This is instead of crashing early unable to gather enough strength and energy for those additional luxuries. This is a positive contributor to your long-term happiness and success. Invest in a juicer as it will pay off in awesome ways.

A shot of Blue Green Algae and a shot of Wheatgrass does a body good. Wheatgrass is a superior detoxifier that contains Chlorophyll. Chlorophyll is a great blood builder. It purifies the liver and decomposes free radicals in the body. This also slows down the aging process. Wheatgrass has many benefits that rid your body of unfriendly bacteria. Chlorophyll also comes in capsule, tablet and powder form. Blue Green Algae is high in nutrients and is a natural energy booster. It contains a high concentration of powerful antioxidants that strengthen the immune system. It also stimulates and aids in the regeneration of damaged body tissues. It also reduces depression symptoms prompting you to be more able to cope with everyday stress. The benefits and effects are evident after regular use.

It is vital that you get at least fifteen to thirty minutes of cardio exercise a day. This can include brisk walking, jogging, biking, running or hiking. Although going for a stroll after a meal is relaxing and allows your body to absorb the fresh air outdoors, this does not meet the daily exercise requirement. Physical activity is important for a myriad of reasons. It raises your vibration so that you can hear the messages and guidance from Heaven more readily. It strengthens your body enabling it to fight off potential illnesses or diseases. It gives you a clear mind and joyful state. All of this attracts in positive circumstances and great luck your way.

With any exercise or health regimen, it is important to consult with a physician to make sure you have no potential issues that could be aggravated by certain exercise routines recommended. You know your own body more than anyone.

Get your soul and your body into shape today. If you have never exercised before, or you rarely exercise, or you have not exercised in a long time, then you will want to ease into a routine with care. This can be something simple such as walking everyday. Move it into a brisk walk. This small bit of exercise will open up the cells in your body and prepare it to increase into stronger physical activity. When my grandmother was in her seventies she was walking briskly up and down hills every single day. When I would see her, I would always ask, "Did you go for your walk today?" If she did not, I would insist that she go. She is now in her eighties at the time of this book and has continued strong health and stamina for her age.

If you did cardio one day, then the next day do some weight training. You know yourself and how much weight you can lift. Both men and women lift weights nowadays in order to strengthen their body. Find the right amount of weight to start with that is safe and works for you. You can increase the weight as you become more accustomed and ready to.

Spirit Guides and Angels

How often do you find yourself thinking about nothing in particular when suddenly a jolt of clear-cut information flies through your mind? What you receive is so commanding you experience a surge of uplifting joy coursing through all of the cells in your body. The idea, key or answer you gained was the missing piece of the puzzle to something you needed to know at that particular time. How many times have you received a nudge to do something that would positively change your life? Instead of taking action on it, you deny it chalking it off to wishful thinking. You later discover that it was indeed an answered prayer, if only you had taken notice and followed the guidance. These are some examples of how you can tell when it is your Spirit Guide or Guardian Angel communicating with you. When you get your lower self and ego out of the way, then that is when the profound answer you had been hoping for is revealed to you. The impression you acquire is so powerful that it pulls you out of the darkness you were previously stuck in. It is a bright light shining its focus directly onto the message in unadorned view. It is crystal clear as if it had been there all along and you wonder why you had not noticed it before.

There are so many joyless faces out there waiting, complaining or praying for a miracle. Instead you choose to fill your days up partaking in activities that only erode your self-esteem and overall well-being. These activities can be something you are not aware of such as sitting in traffic completely tense. You experience another mundane routine day screaming for an escape from this prison of a life you have created. You stay unhappy in your jobs, the places you live in and with certain friendships or relationships. You ponder over not having that home of your dreams or sharing your life with someone in a loving relationship. The days having this dull mindset turn into months and years with no miracle in sight. This disappointment grows like mold causing you to appear and feel eternally glum, negative and bitter. The emotional traits mask your dissatisfaction and heartbreak attracting more of that stuff to you. To cope you drown those nasty emotions with addictions from drinking heavily, ingesting chemicals, doing drugs or by partaking in time wasting activities such as gossip and Internet surfing.

You choose to be disconnected living behind a wall built of your own attitude and yet it is in your basic human nature to want to connect to other human souls, to someone, or something. You want to be happy, but that state can feel so out of reach and unobtainable you drown in its thoughts. Our way of communicating today is primarily through phone, texting, email and social networking. Even if you truly wanted to sit face-to-face you are too busy or worn out to bother. You were not intended to live your life in misery and unhappiness. For some reason, you choose to fall into a pattern of suffering. Human souls as a whole are to blame for this design.

It is never too late to improve your life. What you are looking for is right in front of you and closer than you think. Strengthen your faith and believe in the power of what exists outside of your human body. This will bring you closer to the happiness that resides within. God, your angels, spirit guides and all in Heaven can and want to assist you out of this hopelessness. They are always present around you. They want to lift you out of your life of desolation. It is irrelevant what your beliefs are and whether you are religious or an atheist. It does not matter what race you were born into in this lifetime. Nor does it matter if you are rich or poor, gay or straight, liberal or conservative. Whatever you agreed to come into this lifetime as, you are loved equally. No one is more special than anyone else. God and the angels see each of your inner lights, your innocence and your true purpose for being here. If you have veered long off course, they can help you get back to where you need to be. Who you are is a perfect child of God and love no matter where you are from or who you are.

<u>Raises Vibration</u>

-Exercise
-Healthy Foods
-Surrounding yourself w/ positive people
-Optimism
-Smiling
-Cuddling/Hugging
-Expressing Love
-Praying/Affirmations
-Nature (i.e. relaxing, walking, meditating)
-Music/Singing/Dance
-Grateful/ Gratitude
-Love Relationships
-Breathing techniques
-Water
-Creativity (i.e. art projects)
-Forgiveness
-Compassion
-Experiencing Peace

<u>Lowers Vibration</u>

-Alcohol
-Drugs
-Poor lifestyle choices
-Stress/Depression
-Coffee/Caffeine
-Sugar
-Foods high in fat, sugar, sodium, cholesterol
-Hate/Judgment
-Gossip/Complaining
-Negativity *(i.e. fear, emotion, anger, guilt)*
-Revenge/Gloating
-Unruly Ego
-Being around negative people
-Time Wasters *(i.e. internet surfing, phone apps to meet people, games, bars, clubs)*

Available in paperback and e-book by
Kevin Hunter,
"Warrior of Light: Messages from my Guides and Angels"

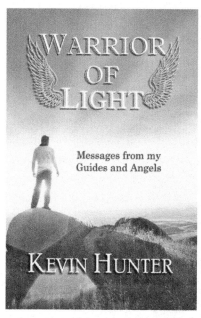

There are legions of angels, spirit guides, and departed loved ones in heaven that watch and guide you on your journey here on Earth. They are around to make your life easier and less stressful. Do you pay attention to the nudges, guidance, and messages given to you? There are many who live lives full of negativity and stress while trying to make ends meet. This can shake your faith as it leads you down paths of addictions, unhealthy life choices, and negative relationship connections. Learn how you can recognize the guidance of your own Spirit team of guides and angels around you. **Author, Kevin Hunter**, relays heavenly guided messages about getting humanity, the world, and yourself into shape. He delivers the guidance passed onto him by his own Spirit team on how to fine tune your body, soul and raise your vibration. Doing this can help you gain hope and faith in your own life in order to start attracting in more abundance

Available in paperback and e-book
by Kevin Hunter,

"Empowering Spirit Wisdom: A Warrior of Light's
Guide on Love, Career and the Spirit World"

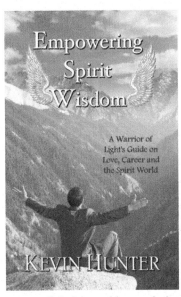

Kevin Hunter relays heavenly, guided messages for everyday life concerns with his book, *Empowering Spirit Wisdom*. Some of the topics covered are your soul, spirit and the power of the light, laws of attraction, finding meaningful work, transforming your professional and personal life, navigating through the various stages of dating and love relationships, as well as other practical affirmations and messages from the Archangels. Kevin Hunter passes on the sensible wisdom given to him by his own Spirit team in this inspirational and powerful book. *Empowering Spirit Wisdom* is part two of the Warrior of Light series of books. Part one is called, *Warrior of Light: Messages from my Guides and Angels.*

In the Spirit Worlds and the dimensions that exist, reside numerous kingdoms that house a plethora of Spirits that inhabit various forms. One of these tribes is called the Wise Ones, a darker breed in the spirit realm who often chooses to incarnate into a human body one lifetime after another for important purposes. The *Realm of the Wise One* takes you on a magical journey to the spirit world where the Wise Ones dwell. This is followed with in-depth and detailed information on how to recognize a human soul who has incarnated from the Wise One Realm. Author, Kevin Hunter, is a Wise One who uses the knowledge passed onto him by his Spirit team of Guides and Angels to relay the wisdom surrounding all things Wise One. He discusses the traits, purposes, gifts, roles, and personalities among other things that make up someone who is a Wise One. Wise Ones have come in the guises of teachers, shaman, leaders, hunters, mediums, entertainers and others. *Realm of the Wise One* is an informational guide devoted to the tribe of the Wise Ones, both in human form and on the other side.

Also available in paperback and e-book by Kevin Hunter,

"Reaching for the Warrior Within"

Reaching for the Warrior Within is the author's personal story recounting a volatile childhood. This led him to a path of addictions, anxiety and overindulgence in alcohol, drugs, cigarettes and destructive relationships. As a survival mechanism, he split into many different "selves". He credits turning his life around, not by therapy, but by simultaneously paying attention to the messages he has been receiving from his Spirit team in Heaven since birth.

Kevin Hunter gains strength, healing and direction with the help of his own team of guides and angels. Living vicariously through this inspiring story will enable you to distinguish when you have been assisted on your own life path. *Reaching for the Warrior Within* attests that anyone can change if they pay attention to their own inner guidance system and take action. This can be from being a victim of child abuse, or a drug and alcohol user, to going after the jobs and relationships you want. This powerful story is for those seeking motivation to change, alter and empower their life one day at a time.

The biggest cause of turmoil and conflict in one's life is executed by the human ego. All souls have an ego. The most unruly and destructive ego exists within every human soul. When the soul enters into a physical human body, the ego immediately compresses and then swells up. It is the higher self's goal to ensure that it remains in check while living an Earthly life. The ego is what tests each soul along its journey. It is how one learns right from wrong. The experiences and challenges that the soul has while living in this Earthly life school contribute to the soul's growth. When a soul learns lessons, it is intended and expected to grow and enhance from the experience. Yet, there are a great many souls who do not learn lessons and remain in the same spot. The ill of the bunch wreaks all kinds of havoc, destruction, judgment and heart ache in its wake. In *Darkness of Ego*, author Kevin Hunter infuses some of the guidance, messages, and wisdom he's received from his Spirit team surrounding all things ego related. The ego is one of the most damaging culprits in human life. Therefore it is essential to understand the nature of the beast in order to navigate gracefully out of it when it spins out of control. Some of the topics covered in *Darkness of Ego* are humanity's destruction, mass hysteria, karmic debt, and the power of the mind, heaven's gate, the ego's war on love and relationships, and much more.

The *Warrior of Light* series of mini-pocket books are available in paperback and E-book by Kevin Hunter called, *Spirit Guides and Angels, Soul Mates and Twin Flames, Divine Messages for Humanity, Raising Your Vibration, Connecting with the Archangels*

Also available in paperback and E-book by Kevin Hunter, *Ignite Your Inner Life Force*, *Awaken Your Creative Spirit* and *The Seven Deadly Sins*

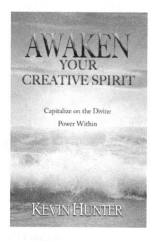

ABOUT THE AUTHOR

Kevin Hunter is an author, love expert and channeler. His books tackle a variety of genres and tend to have a strong male protagonist. The messages and themes he weaves in his work surround Spirit's own communications of love and respect which he channels and infuses into his writing and stories.

His books include the *Warrior of Light series of books, Warrior of Light, Empowering Spirit Wisdom, Realm of the Wise One, Reaching for the Warrior Within, Darkness of Ego, Ignite Your Inner Life Force, Awaken Your Creative Spirit,* and *The Seven Deadly Sins.* He is also the author of the horror, drama, *Paint the Silence*, and the modern day erotic love story, *Jagger's Revolution.*

Before writing books and stories, Kevin started out in the entertainment business in 1996 becoming actress Michelle Pfeiffer's personal development dude for her boutique production company, Via Rosa Productions. She dissolved her company after several years and he made a move into coordinating film productions for the big studios on such films as *One Fine Day, A Thousand Acres, The Deep End of the Ocean, Crazy in Alabama, Original Sin, The Perfect Storm, Harry Potter & the Sorcerer's Stone, Dr. Dolittle 2* and *Carolina.* He considers himself a beach bum born and raised in Los Angeles, California.

For more information, www.kevin-hunter.com